hamlyn

Pasta

Joanna Farrow

Notes

Ovens should be preheated to the specified temperature. If using a fan-assisted oven, follow the manufacturer's instructions for adjusting the time and temperature. Grills should also be preheated.

This book includes dishes made with nuts and nut derivatives. It is advisable for those with known allergic reactions to nuts and nut derivatives and those who may be potentially vulnerable to these allergies, such as pregnant women and nursing mothers, invalids, the elderly, babies and children, to avoid dishes made with nuts and nut oils. It is also prudent to check the labels of preprepared ingredients for the possible inclusion of nut derivatives.

The Department of Health advises that eggs should not be consumed raw. This book contains some dishes made with raw or lightly cooked eggs. It is prudent for more vulnerable people, such as pregnant women and nursing mothers, invalids, the elderly, babies and young children to avoid uncooked or lightly cooked dishes made with eggs.

Fresh herbs should be used unless otherwise stated. If unavailable use dried herbs as an alternative but halve the quantities stated.

Meat and poultry should be cooked thoroughly. To test if poultry is cooked, pierce the flesh through the thickest part with a skewer or fork – the juices should run clear, never pink or red.

First published in Great Britain in 2007 by
Hamlyn, a division of Octopus Publishing Group Ltd
2–4 Heron Quays, London E14 4JP

Copyright © Octopus Publishing Group Ltd 2007

ISBN-13: 978-0-600-61596-5
ISBN-10: 0-600-61596-0

A CIP catalogue record for this book is available from the British Library

Printed and bound in China

10 9 8 7 6 5 4 3 2 1

Contents

Introduction

Pasta is one of the most infinitely versatile foods imaginable. Whether it's shop-bought fresh or dried, or a homemade labour of love, it can form the basis of the quickest midweek supper or satisfy the more demanding expectations of the smartest dinner party with friends.

Versatility

The various shapes and types of fresh and dried pasta available are as diverse as the range of dishes you can cook with them. Becoming familiar with them all is almost impossible because there are so many regional variations throughout Italy. In general, northern Italy tends to use fresh egg pasta and stuffed pasta dishes served with butter, cream and cheese sauces, whereas southern Italy is better known for its firm-textured dried pasta. Sweet, full-flavoured tomato sauces are most often used to partner this type of pasta.

Many of the recipes in this book use familiar pasta shapes, such as tagliatelle, penne and fusilli, but some incorporate more unusual shapes, such as conchiglie (shells), orecchiette (little ears) and garganelli (scroll-shaped pasta). The great thing about cooking pasta, though, is its versatility. If you can't manage to find a particular pasta shape, then using another similar one won't spoil a recipe. The most important element is to get the cooking just right and serve the pasta promptly. Cooked pasta spoils very quickly if it's left hanging around.

Types of pasta

Neither fresh nor dried pasta is superior. It's a question of personal taste and how you intend to use it. A useful guide, if you're unsure when buying, is to choose your pasta from the Italian brands or from quality supermarket brands, sourced from Italian factories.

Dried pasta Sometimes commercially available dried pasta is made with egg, called 'pasta all'uovo', but it is often made without, particularly in the southern Italian specialities, such as orecchiette. Always buy dried pasta that's made from durum wheat, often labelled 'semola' in Italian. Because dried pasta is usually machine made it comes in many different shapes that you can't necessarily make at home or buy as fresh pasta. The three main types of dried pasta are **long pasta**, which includes tagliatelle, spaghetti, linguine and pappardelle, sometimes bought in little nest shapes. **Short pasta** includes the vast array of pasta shapes, including rigatoni, conchiglie and farfalle. Very small pasta shapes, such as stelline and orzo, are usually added to soups. **Flat pasta** refers to lasagne sheets, which can also be rolled around a filling, as in cannelloni.

Fresh pasta Fresh pasta is made using eggs and a soft wheat '00' flour, which gives it its silky smooth, soft texture. Supermarkets stock a reasonable selection of fresh pastas, but if you have the time and just a little patience it's well worth making your own because homemade pasta has a 'freshly made' texture that's more like the sort you buy from Italian delicatessens, which are, naturally, also very good sources. Flavoured pastas are becoming increasingly widely used, from traditional ones such as tomato, spinach and squid ink to the more adventurous, such as chilli, cracked pepper and beetroot.

The long, short and flat fresh pastas are available in many of the same forms as the dried, although not in such a diverse range. **Stuffed pastas**, filled with vegetable, cheese, fish or meaty fillings, make an exciting and increasingly popular addition to the fresh pasta choice and can be thoroughly rewarding to make at home.

Equipment for making and cooking pasta *The only absolutely essential items needed for cooking pasta are a large saucepan and a decent sized colander for draining. If you're keen to make your own pasta, there are some additional pieces of equipment you might find useful.*

Pasta machine There are two types of pasta machine. The elaborate electric pasta maker, which mixes, kneads and extrudes pasta to various shapes, is very expensive and needs plenty of storage space. For most domestic kitchens, and certainly for the purposes of the recipes in this book, a small hand-cranked pasta machine for rolling and cutting is ideal. It rolls the pasta very thinly to flat sheets and can also be used to shape wide and fine ribbon noodles. Made of stainless steel, it's easy to wipe clean and should last for years, making it an inexpensive and durable investment for keen pasta makers.

Pasta wheel This small, hand-held tool has a plain or fluted wheel for cutting broad noodles, such as pappardelle, or stuffed pasta shapes, such as ravioli. Some come with multiple wheels so you can cut several lengths at the same time.

Ravioli cutter This small gadget, which may be round or square, plain or fluted, has a wooden handle and is used for stamping out pasta shapes such as tortellini and ravioli. You can use small metal or plastic biscuit cutters instead.

Ravioli tin This is a sectioned metal tray with small cavities set in a raised, serrated grid, designed to speed up the process of ravioli making. It's particularly useful for shaping small ravioli squares, which would otherwise be very time consuming and fiddly. To use the tin, line it with a sheet of thinly rolled pasta dough, pressing it into the dips in the tin. Spoon in the filling, brush the pasta with water and cover with a second sheet of pasta before rolling the top with a rolling pin, which separates the squares between the serrated lines.

Tapered rolling pin This is a very long, thin wooden rolling pin, which is tapered at the ends and used for hand-rolling pasta sheets. You can use an ordinary rolling pin, preferably a long and slender one, instead.

Pasta saucepan This large saucepan comes with an inner, perforated draining basket, which can be lifted out once the pasta is cooked for quick and easy draining. Alternatively, you can use an ordinary large saucepan and drain the pasta through a large colander.

Pasta tongs Used for lifting and serving long pasta, the tongs have prongs that grip the pasta and stop it slipping and sliding back into the pan.

Pasta dryers These are used for hanging homemade flat ribbon pasta for drying. Available in a wood or plastic finish, the dryer comes with a series of rods, which swivel out from a stand so that plenty of pasta can be dried in one go.

Basic pasta dough

This quantity is sufficient for 4 servings as part of a meal. If making stuffed pasta, where there's more wastage, you can increase the ingredients to 300 g (10 oz) flour and 3 large eggs.

PREPARATION TIME: 15 minutes, plus standing, rolling and shaping

SERVES: 4 as a main course, 6–8 as a starter

200 g (7 oz) '00' grade flour, plus extra for dusting

2 large eggs

1 Tip the flour out on to the work surface and make a well in the centre. (Working directly on the work surface is the traditional and easiest way of mixing pasta dough, but if you feel uncertain about working on the surface, use a mixing bowl.)

2 Break the eggs into the well. Beat the eggs lightly with a fork and, as you beat, gradually start to blend the flour into the eggs. When the eggs are thickened with flour, push the rest of the flour over the eggs and mix the whole lot together to make a crumbly paste.

3 Continue to work the mixture to a dough, sprinkling in more flour if the dough starts sticking to the surface. Pasta dough should feel firmer and more compact than bread or pastry dough but not so firm that it's leathery and unsupple.

4 Knead the dough until it is smooth and elastic, then wrap it in clingfilm and leave to stand at room temperature for 20 minutes. This will relax the dough and make it easier to roll and shape.

Tip If you really can't manage to get hold of pasta '00' flour, then use strong white bread flour instead.

Using and storing dough

Pasta dough has to be rolled out before it can be shaped, either by hand or machine. Once you've made your chosen pasta it can be stored in the refrigerator for a few hours, or frozen or dried for longer storage.

Rolling out the dough

Line two or three baking sheets or trays with tea towels or kitchen paper and lightly dust them with flour. Divide the dough into six wedges (or 8–10 wedges if you are working with a larger quantity).

Using a pasta machine Flatten a piece of dough into an oval shape that's slightly narrower than the machine rollers and dust generously with flour. Set the machine to its widest setting and roll the pasta through the machine. Reset the machine to a slightly narrower setting, fold the pasta in half lengthways, dust with flour and run it through again. Roll the pasta through the machine once or twice more, each time setting the machine to a narrower setting, until it is 1–2 mm (about 1/16 inch) thick. (You probably won't need to go to the narrowest setting on the machine because the pasta will be too thin to use.) If necessary, cut the pasta lengths in half to make them more manageable. Lay the rolled sheets on the lined baking sheets or trays while rolling the remainder.

Shaping by hand Dust the dough, work surface and rolling pin with flour and roll out the dough as thinly as possible.

Storing pasta

Fresh pasta dough can be stored for several hours in the refrigerator, wrapped in clingfilm. Once rolled and shaped, it will keep in the refrigerator for several hours or overnight. Stuffed pasta doesn't keep as long as flat pasta because the stuffing can soften the dough and make it sticky. This is best cooked within 4–6 hours of shaping. For longer storage (up to a month), freeze the shapes in a rigid container, interleaving the layers with clingfilm.

Drying Cut the pasta to the chosen shape or width (see page 10) and lay the pieces on the floured tea towels or paper. Leave to dry for 30 minutes before cooking.

Any long pasta can easily be dried for storage of up to 6–8 weeks. Hang the pasta lengths over a pole suspended across the work surface or use a special pasta drying rack. As soon as the pasta is dry and brittle, which usually takes about 24 hours, wrap it loosely in polythene bags and store in a cool, dry place.

Lasagne Cut lasagne to convenient-sized sheets. If rolled in the machine, the sheets can be left at this width and then cut into 15–20 cm (6–8 inch) lengths.

Cannelloni This is cut in the same way as lasagne, ready for rolling around meat or vegetable fillings.

Pappardelle These are the broadest noodles, usually 2–3 cm ($^3/_4$–1$^1/_4$ inches) wide. Cut the rolled dough into strips with a fluted pasta or pastry wheel or a knife.

Tagliatelle Cut the sheets of pasta to about 30 cm (12 inches) in length to make them more manageable. Flour the pasta and fold it over several times. Cut the pasta into strips about 5–10 mm ($^1/_4$–$^1/_2$ inch) wide. Unroll the pasta to separate the layers. Alternatively, shape the pasta by running it through the tagliatelle cutter of the pasta machine.

Fettuccine These are a slightly narrower type of ribbon noodle. Use the same method as for tagliatelle, but cut the noodles 3 mm (just under $^1/_4$ inch) thick. Fettuccine can also be cut using the pasta machine.

Linguine Use the same method as for tagliatelle, but cut the noodles as finely as possible, preferably using a pasta machine.

Farfalle Use a knife to cut the pasta sheets into 5 x 3 cm (2 x 1$^1/_4$ inch) rectangles. Firmly squeeze the two long sides of each rectangle together to make a bow-tie shape.

Quadrucci Cut the pasta into 3–4 cm (1$^1/_4$–1$^1/_2$ inch) strips then cut them across into squares. This is a flat pasta shape traditionally used in soups.

Flavoured pasta

Flavoured pastas can be bought fresh or dried, or made at home. The taste can be quite subtle, but they do add a fabulous colour to a pasta dish. The following flavour variations are used for a 200 g (7 oz) quantity of flour (see page 8).

Spinach Cook 100 g (3^1/$_2$ oz) spinach leaves in a saucepan with a splash of water until wilted. Drain the spinach and squeeze it dry in your hands to remove as much moisture as possible. Dry it further by pressing between several sheets of kitchen paper. Blend in a food processor with one of the eggs, then mix with the remaining egg and make as for plain pasta. The dough will be stickier than a plain pasta dough because of the moisture in the spinach, so you'll need to work in a little extra flour.

Tomato Add 3 tablespoons sun-dried tomato paste to the eggs before working in the flour. Add a little extra flour when kneading if the dough feels sticky.

Mushroom Cover 15 g (^{1}/$_2$ oz) dried porcini mushrooms with boiling water and leave for 15 minutes. Drain, reserving 2 teaspoons of the juice. Blend the mushrooms and reserved juice in a food processor to make a paste and mix with the eggs before working in the flour. Add extra flour if the dough feels sticky.

Cracked pepper Whisk 4 teaspoons freshly ground black pepper into the eggs before working in the flour.

Chilli Whisk ^{3}/$_4$ teaspoon hot chilli powder into the eggs before working in the flour.

Herb Finely chop 25 g (1 oz) of a single herb or mixed herbs. Flat leaf parsley, dill, fennel, coriander, basil, thyme and tarragon are all suitable, but make sure they're thoroughly dry before chopping. Whisk into the eggs before working in the flour.

Saffron Finely crumble 1 teaspoon saffron threads and whisk into the eggs before working in the flour.

Beetroot Cook 100 g (3^1/$_2$ oz) whole beetroot in water until tender. Skin, roughly chop and blend in a food processor with one of the eggs. Strain through a sieve and add to the remaining egg.

Squid ink Whisk 5 g (^{1}/$_4$ oz) squid ink into the eggs before working in the flour. The dough will be stickier than a plain pasta dough, so you'll need to work in a little extra flour.

Stuffed pasta

The best-known stuffed pasta is ravioli, but homemade agnolotti, tortellini and cappelletti are equally achievable. Once made, put the stuffed pasta on a floured tea towel and leave to dry for about 30 minutes before cooking. Stuffed pastas can also be stored in the refrigerator for several hours or frozen for up to a month, layered between sheets of clingfilm.

Preparation Before you start, have your chosen filling ready and cooled, if it's a cooked one. (See the recipes on pages 34, 88 and 113 for filling suggestions.) Line a couple of large baking sheets or trays with floured tea towels or kitchen paper. Roll out the pasta sheets by hand or using the machine, so you end up with plenty of thin, even sized sheets (see page 9).

Don't discard the trimmings; cut them into even-sized pieces and add to soups, or cook and toss with sauces.

Ravioli Ravioli is usually cut to about 5 cm (2 inch) squares, but once you're familiar with the technique, you can experiment with mini ravioli – about 3 cm (1¼ inches) square, large ones – about 8.5 cm (3½ inches) square, or rounds (see below). Special ravioli tins are useful for making a large amount of ravioli (see page 7), but it's really very easy, and rewarding, to make ravioli by hand.

Put a pasta sheet on a floured work surface. Place scant teaspoonfuls of the filling in a line, at 2.5 cm (1 inch) intervals, down the length of the dough and flatten them slightly. If the pasta strip is wide enough, add more spoonfuls of filling, making sure there is a 2.5 cm (1 inch) gap between each. Using a pastry brush dipped in a little water, lightly brush the pasta all around the piles of filling. Loosely lay another sheet of pasta on top. Working from one end, press the dough down between the mounds, sealing the filling firmly in the pasta and excluding all the air. Use a knife or ravioli cutter to cut the ravioli into squares between the mounds. Transfer to the floured tea towels or paper while you make the remainder.

To make round ravioli, make as above and cut out rounds using a plain or fluted ravioli or biscuit cutter.

Agnolotti Cut a rolled strip of pasta to 5 cm (2 inches) wide. Place scant $^1/_2$ teaspoons of filling along the centre of the strip, leaving a 3 cm ($1^1/_4$ inch) space between each. Using a pastry brush dipped in a little water, lightly brush the pasta all around the piles of filling. Fold the pasta over so the filling sits against the fold. Press the pasta down firmly around each mound, excluding any air. Use a 5 cm (2 inch) fluted ravioli or biscuit cutter to cut out crescent shapes around the stuffing. Transfer to the floured tea towels while you make the remainder.

Tortellini Using a 7–8 cm ($2^3/_4$–3 inch) plain or fluted ravioli or biscuit cutter, cut out rounds from the dough. Place a scant teaspoon of filling in the centre of each. Using a pastry brush dipped in a little water, lightly brush the pasta all around the filling. Fold over one side of the dough and press together firmly, excluding the air. Bring the ends together around the filling and pinch firmly to seal. Transfer to the floured tea towel while you make the remainder.

Cappelletti These are made in a similar way to tortellini except that the shapes are cut into squares, which are folded diagonally across the filling. Pinch the two folded corners together to make little hat shapes.

Cooking perfect pasta

Cooking pasta is very easy. The main consideration is having the sauces and accompaniments ready to serve as soon as the pasta is cooked. If it is left to stand, the pasta will continue cooking in its own steam and start to stick together.

Dried pasta Bring a large saucepan or pasta pan (see page 7) of water to the boil. As a guide, allow about 4 litres (7 pints) water to 300 g (10 oz) pasta. This large quantity of water is essential for cooking the pasta quickly and stopping the pieces sticking together. Sprinkle in plenty of salt and return the water to a rolling boil, then add the pasta, all in one go. Return the water to the boil, giving the pasta an occasional stir to stop it sticking together. If you are cooking long pasta, such as spaghetti, hold it at one end and press it down into the boiling water, pushing it in further as it softens. Once it is submerged, stir with a wooden spoon to separate the strands.

After cooking, drain the pasta and return it to the pan for piling on to serving plates or tossing with a sauce. When draining, always leave a little water clinging to the pasta. This keeps it moist and any sauces it's tossed with won't be sucked into the pasta, giving dry results.

Italians use the term *al dente*, meaning firm to the bite, to describe the texture dried pasta should have when it is cooked. Test by lifting a little pasta from the water, using tongs or a fork, towards the end of the recommended cooking time. It should be tender but still retain a little bite in the centre. As a guide, most pasta shapes and long pasta take 8–12 minutes to cook; small pasta shapes might take only about 5 minutes to cook; and very fine pasta, such as vermicelli, will take only 2–3 minutes. These are very approximate times because it will vary according to the brand and how long the pasta has been stored.

Fresh pasta Use the same method as above but remember that fresh pasta cooks very quickly and is easy to overcook. Once added to the pan and returned to the boil it can be ready in seconds rather than minutes, so keep checking as it boils. Fresh pasta has a much softer texture than dried and is more prone to breaking up once it is cooked, so drain and serve it carefully. Bear in mind that fresh homemade pasta will probably cook more quickly than fresh commercial pasta.

Gnocchi

This is not a true pasta but shares many similarities in the way it is prepared and cooked. It can be made several hours in advance if stored in the refrigerator.

PREPARATION TIME: 30 minutes

COOKING TIME: 45 minutes

SERVES: 4

750 g (1½ lb) medium, floury potatoes
40 g (1½ oz) Parmesan cheese, grated
125–150 g (4–5 oz) plain flour
salt

1 Put the potatoes, whole and unpeeled, in a saucepan and cover with water. Bring to the boil and boil for about 40 minutes until tender. (Try not to pierce them too often with a fork, or the potatoes will absorb too much water.) Drain and peel the potatoes as soon as they're cool enough to handle.

2 Return the potatoes to the cleaned pan and mash until smooth, then beat in the Parmesan and a little salt. Add 100 g (3½ oz) of the flour, beating with a wooden spoon until smooth. When the mixture becomes too dry to mix, turn it out on to the work surface and knead in a little more flour with your hands. Stop working in the flour when the mixture makes a soft dough that's only slightly sticky. Divide into 4 pieces and roll each under the palms of your hands to a long rope about 1.5 cm (¾ inch) thick. Cut these into 2.5 cm (1 inch) long pieces.

3 Take a piece of gnocchi and press it on to the tines of a floured fork, pressing an indentation into the other side with your finger and rolling the gnocchi slightly to make it into a curved shape. Repeat with the remaining pieces.

4 Bring a large saucepan of salted water to the boil and boil the gnocchi, in batches, for about 2 minutes until they rise to the surface. Lift out the gnocchi with a slotted spoon and drain thoroughly.

Introduction 15

Starters, snacks and salads *This chapter contains a wide variety of recipes that are infinitely adaptable. It combines many ingredients we associate with starters, such as smoked salmon, asparagus, crab and Parma ham, with various types of pasta. Packed into shells, stuffed in ravioli or wrapped in crumpled lasagne, they're appetizingly presented and delicious, but fairly substantial and therefore best served prior to a reasonably light main course.*

The soups serve equally well as starters (in small portions) or as warming, robust supper dishes. Served this way, the cooking time of the pasta isn't quite so crucial and the dishes can even be reheated the next day.

The salads too are adaptable: simply adjust portion sizes depending on whether there are other courses to follow. Colourful and fresh tasting, these salads are good for transporting, either in lunchboxes or to picnics, in which case drizzle with any dressing just before you leave home or shortly before eating.

Minestrone

There are many regional variations on minestrone, and this recipe combines elements of them all. You can use all sorts of vegetable odds and ends. It also reheats well the next day.

PREPARATION TIME: 20 minutes

COOKING TIME: 1½ hours

SERVES: 6

2 tablespoons olive oil, plus extra for drizzling

1 onion, chopped

3 carrots, chopped

3 celery sticks, chopped

2 garlic cloves, thinly sliced

400 g (13 oz) can cannellini beans, drained and rinsed

400 g (13 oz) can plum tomatoes or 6 fresh tomatoes, skinned and chopped

150 g (5 oz) peas or broad beans

1 large potato, diced

2 courgettes, diced

1.5 litres (2½ pints) chicken or vegetable stock

150 g (5 oz) cavolo nero, shredded, or spinach

75 g (3 oz) small dried pasta shapes

salt and pepper

TO SERVE
grated Parmesan or pecorino cheese

homemade or bought pesto

1 Heat the oil in a large saucepan and gently fry the onion, carrots and celery for 5 minutes. Add the garlic and fry for a further 2 minutes.

2 Add the beans, tomatoes, peas or beans, potato, courgettes and stock to the pan and bring gently to a simmer. Cover with a lid and simmer gently for about 1 hour or until all the vegetables are tender.

3 Add the shredded cavolo nero or spinach to the pan. Scatter in the pasta and stir gently. Cover and cook for a further 10 minutes or until the pasta is cooked through. Check the seasoning

4 Ladle into shallow bowls, drizzle with extra olive oil and serve with the grated Parmesan or pecorino and pesto.

Butter bean, pesto and broccoli soup *A few spoonfuls of pesto, homemade or bought, are enough to transform the most basic mixture of ingredients into a real treat.*

PREPARATION TIME: 15 minutes

COOKING TIME: 25–30 minutes

SERVES: 4

3 tablespoons olive oil

1 onion, finely chopped

1 litre (1¾ pints) vegetable or chicken stock

400 g (13 oz) can butter beans, rinsed and drained

½ quantity, about 150 g (5 oz), Basil and Pine Nut Pesto (see page 67)

200 g (7 oz) broccoli, cut into small florets

125 g (4 oz) small fresh or dried pasta shapes, or homemade soup pasta, such as quadrucci (see page 10)

salt and pepper

1 Heat the oil in a saucepan and fry the onion for 5 minutes until softened. Add the stock and beans and bring to the boil. Reduce the heat and cook gently for 10 minutes.

2 Stir in the pesto, broccoli and dried pasta shapes. If you are using fresh pasta, add it to the pan once the broccoli has started to soften.

3 Cook very gently for a couple of minutes, or until the pasta is cooked through, then check the seasoning and serve.

Pasta in broth

Pasta cooked in broth can be as simple or elaborate as you like. Use your own specially made stuffed meat or cheese pasta, or cheat and buy ready made for a speedy supper dish.

PREPARATION TIME: 10 minutes

COOKING TIME: 20 minutes

SERVES: 4

2 tablespoons olive oil

1 small onion, finely chopped

1 celery stick, finely chopped

several sprigs of thyme

1 small glass of white wine

1.5 litres (2½ pints) vegetable, chicken or beef stock

200 g (7 oz) fresh ravioli, tortellini or cappelletti

2–3 tablespoons finely chopped parsley or basil

salt and pepper

grated or shaved Parmesan, to serve

1 Heat the oil in a large saucepan and gently fry the onion, celery and thyme for 5 minutes.

2 Add the wine and stock and bring slowly to the boil. Reduce the heat and cook gently, uncovered, for 5 minutes.

3 Return the broth to the boil and drop in the pasta. Cook for 5 minutes. Test by draining one piece and cutting it in half. The pasta should be just tender and the filling cooked through.

4 Stir in the parsley or basil and season to taste with salt and pepper. Ladle the broth into bowls and serve sprinkled with plenty of Parmesan.

Chicken, ginger and vermicelli broth

This is a good recipe to try when you're left with a large chicken carcass and a bit of leftover meat from a roast dinner.

PREPARATION TIME: 15 minutes

COOKING TIME: 1 hour 20 minutes

SERVES: 4–6

carcass and leftover meat from a large roasted chicken, plus any jellied juices

2 onions

350 g (11½ oz) carrots

3 bay leaves

several sprigs of rosemary or thyme

50 g (2 oz) fresh root ginger, peeled and grated

200 g (7 oz) fresh or frozen peas

150 g (5 oz) fresh or dried vermicelli

salt and pepper

1 Remove the meat left on the carcass, shred it into small pieces and reserve. Pack the carcass into a saucepan into which it fits quite snugly and add any juices. Cut one onion into wedges, leaving the skin on for colour.

2 Roughly slice half the carrots. Add the onion wedges and sliced carrots to the pan with the herbs and just cover the ingredients with cold water.

3 Bring the carcass to the boil, then reduce the heat to a very gentle simmer and cook, half covered with a lid, for 1 hour. Strain the stock through a colander into a clean pan.

4 Finely chop the remaining onion and slice the remaining carrots. Add to the pan with the ginger and cook gently for about 10 minutes or until the vegetables are tender.

5 Add the peas, reserved chicken meat and vermicelli. Cook for 6–8 minutes or until the vermicelli is tender. Check the seasoning and serve.

Chicken, mangetout and peach salad

This salad is a delicious concoction of complimentary colours and flavours, from sweet and juicy peaches to the saltiness of the dressing.

PREPARATION TIME: 15 minutes

COOKING TIME: 10 minutes

SERVES: 4

200 g (7 oz) dried pasta shapes, such as rigatoni, lumaconi or trompretti

125 g (4 oz) mangetout, sliced diagonally

2 large, juicy peaches

200 g (7 oz) lean, cooked chicken, roughly sliced

½ bunch of spring onions, sliced diagonally

15 g (½ oz) coriander leaves, chopped

salt and pepper

DRESSING:

3 tablespoons clear honey

3 tablespoons lemon juice

4 tablespoons mild olive oil

1 tablespoon soy sauce

2 teaspoons Thai fish sauce

1 Bring a large saucepan of salted water to the boil, add the pasta and cook for 8–10 minutes until just tender. Add the mangetout and cook for a further 1 minute. Drain and rinse under cold running water. Drain thoroughly and turn into a large bowl.

2 Halve, stone and thinly slice the peaches and add them to the bowl with the chicken, spring onions and coriander.

3 Make the dressing by whisking together the honey, lemon juice, olive oil, soy sauce and Thai fish sauce.

4 Just before serving, pour the dressing over the salad, season with pepper and toss the ingredients together well.

Frazzled squid and pasta salad

Cooling cucumber, crispy fried squid and fresh herbs make this salad visually stunning and full of flavour. Serve with a large pasta shape, such as rigatoni.

PREPARATION TIME: 25 minutes

COOKING TIME: 15 minutes

SERVES: 4–6

½ cucumber, peeled and sliced

1 tablespoon salt, plus extra for cooking

200 g (3½ oz) dried pasta shapes

100 g (5 oz) rocket

100 ml (3½ fl oz) olive oil

500 g (1 lb) small squid

1 teaspoon ground paprika

1 tablespoon plain flour

1–2 tablespoons lemon juice

1 teaspoon caster sugar

40 g (1½ oz) mixed herbs, such as parsley, chives, basil and fennel

pepper

1 Layer the cucumber in a small colander, sprinkling each layer lightly with the salt.

2 Bring a large saucepan of salted water to the boil. Add the pasta, return to the boil and cook for 10 minutes or until just tender. Drain and tip into a bowl. Add the rocket and 1 tablespoon oil and toss the ingredients together.

3 Rinse the squid, halve lengthways and pat dry on kitchen paper. (If the tentacles are present, cut these from the heads and use as well.) Toss the paprika with the flour and coat the squid. Heat another 2 tablespoons oil and fry the squid for 4–5 minutes until golden. Drain.

4 Put the remaining oil in a blender with 1 tablespoon lemon juice, the sugar, herbs and pepper. Blend until finely chopped.

5 Rinse the cucumber in several changes of cold water to remove the salt, and drain. Add to the pasta with the squid and dressing. Mix together and drizzle with a little extra lemon juice, if needed.

Chilli and prawn fusilli with basil yogurt

There are two dressings with this salad – a sweet, spicy chilli sauce and a contrasting, cooling basil and yogurt dressing.

PREPARATION TIME: 20 minutes

COOKING TIME: 3–10 minutes

SERVES: 4–6

200 g (7 oz) fresh or dried plain or tomato-flavoured fusilli or farfalle

5 tablespoons mild olive oil or groundnut oil

2 spring onions

3 tablespoons sweet chilli sauce

1 tablespoon lemon juice

3 tablespoons sun-dried tomato paste

1 teaspoon caster sugar

250 g (8 oz) freshly cooked peeled prawns

100 g (3½ oz) bottled sweet peppers, drained and sliced

25 g (1 oz) finely shredded basil leaves

150 g (5 oz) natural yogurt

salt

1 Bring a large saucepan of salted water to the boil. Add the pasta, return to the boil and cook, allowing 3 minutes for fresh pasta and 8–10 minutes for dried. Drain and toss in a bowl with 1 tablespoon oil.

2 Trim the spring onions and finely chop, keeping the white part separate from the green. Mix the white spring onions in a small bowl with the chilli sauce, lemon juice, tomato paste, sugar and the remaining oil.

3 Add the mixture to the pasta with the prawns and sliced peppers and mix well together. Turn into a shallow serving dish.

4 Mix the basil with the green parts of the spring onions and the yogurt. Spoon over the salad just before serving.

Garganelli with roasted cherry tomatoes *This fresh, summery salad is tossed in a herby, Mediterranean-style sauce, which is delicious with the roasted tomatoes.*

PREPARATION TIME: 15 minutes

COOKING TIME: 40 minutes

SERVES: 4–6

200 g (7 oz) cherry tomatoes, halved

2 teaspoons chopped thyme

½ teaspoon caster sugar

150 ml (¼ pint) olive oil

200 g (7 oz) fresh or dried garganelli

2 teaspoons coriander seeds

1 teaspoon mustard seeds

25 g (1 oz) chopped herbs, such as chervil, tarragon, flat leaf parsley or chives

1 garlic clove, crushed

finely grated rind of 1 lime, plus 2 tablespoons juice

3 tablespoons capers, drained and rinsed

salt and pepper

1 Scatter the tomatoes, cut sides up, in a single layer in a roasting tin. Sprinkle with the thyme, sugar, 2 tablespoons oil and a little salt and pepper. Roast in a preheated oven, 200°C (400°F), Gas Mark 6, for about 40 minutes or until the tomatoes are soft and browned around the edges.

2 Meanwhile, bring a large saucepan of salted water to the boil. Add the pasta, return to the boil and cook, allowing 3 minutes for fresh pasta and 8–10 minutes for dried. Drain and toss in a bowl with 1 tablespoon oil.

3 Use a pestle and mortar to crush the coriander and mustard seeds. Tip them into a small saucepan with the remaining oil, herbs, garlic, lime rind and juice and a little salt and pepper and warm through gently for 2–3 minutes to get the flavours mingling.

4 Scatter the roasted tomatoes and capers over the pasta and pour over the dressing. Toss the salad together and chill until ready to serve.

Linguine with shredded ham and eggs

This recipe is put together in minutes and is conveniently adaptable. Use other shredded, cooked meats instead of the ham if you prefer.

PREPARATION TIME: 5 minutes

COOKING TIME: 10 minutes

SERVES: 2

125 g (4 oz) dried linguine

3 tablespoons chopped flat leaf parsley

1 tablespoon coarse grain mustard

2 teaspoons lemon juice

good pinch of caster sugar

3 tablespoons olive oil

100 g (3½ oz) thinly sliced ham

2 spring onions

2 eggs

salt and pepper

1 Bring a saucepan of salted water to the boil to cook the pasta. Meanwhile, mix together the parsley, mustard, lemon juice, sugar, oil and a little salt and pepper. Roll up the ham and slice it as thinly as possible. Trim the spring onions, cut them lengthways into thin shreds, then cut into 5 cm (2 inch) lengths.

2 Put the eggs in a small saucepan and just cover with cold water. Bring to the boil and cook for 4 minutes (once the water boils the eggs will usually start to move around).

3 Put the pasta in the salted water, return to the boil and boil for 6–8 minutes or until just tender. Add the spring onions and cook for a further 30 seconds.

4 Drain the pasta and return to the pan. Stir in the ham and the mustard dressing and pile on to warm serving plates. Shell and halve the eggs and serve on top.

Linguine with shredded ham and eggs

Chorizo and saffron agnolotti *These pretty little Mediterranean-inspired pasta shapes might be a bit fiddly, but they are a brilliant make-ahead starter.*

PREPARATION TIME: 50 minutes, plus drying

COOKING TIME: 10 minutes

SERVES: 6

200 g (7 oz) chorizo sausage, roughly chopped

100 g (3½ oz) buffalo mozzarella cheese, roughly chopped

3 tablespoons sun-dried tomato paste

1 teaspoon finely chopped oregano

1 quantity saffron-flavoured pasta dough (see page 11)

flour for dusting

1 quantity Fresh Tomato Sauce (see page 66)

small oregano leaves, to garnish

salt and pepper

1 Put the the chorizo and mozzarella in a food processor with the tomato paste, oregano and a little salt and pepper. Blend to a paste.

2 Line 2 trays with flour-dusted tea towels or kitchen paper. Roll out the pasta, using a machine or by hand following the method on page 9. Use the chorizo mixture and rolled pasta to make agnolotti, following the method on page 13. Leave on the floured trays to dry for 30 minutes before cooking.

3 Bring a large saucepan of salted water to the boil. Add half the agnolotti, return to the boil and cook for 5 minutes. Drain with a slotted spoon and cook the remainder.

4 Meanwhile, reheat the tomato sauce in a saucepan. Spoon the sauce on to warm serving plates and pile the pasta on top. Spoon over a little more sauce and serve scattered with oregano leaves.

Pappardelle with figs, gorgonzola and Parma ham

This recipe combines sweet and salty flavours, tossed in a honey and orange dressing. Serve for a light lunch or a simple starter.

PREPARATION TIME: 10 minutes

COOKING TIME: 2–10 minutes

SERVES: 4–6

200 g (7 oz) fresh or dried pappardelle

2 tablespoons clear honey

2 teaspoons coarse grain mustard

3 tablespoons freshly squeezed orange juice

squeeze of lemon juice

3 tablespoons mild olive oil

4 ripe, juicy figs, cut into thin wedges

100 g (3½ oz) Parma ham, torn into small pieces

150 g (5 oz) Gorgonzola cheese, roughly diced

salt and pepper

1 Bring a large saucepan of salted water to the boil. Add the pasta, return to the boil and cook, allowing 2–3 minutes for fresh and 8–10 minutes for dried.

2 Meanwhile, whisk together the honey, mustard, orange and lemon juice, oil and a little salt and pepper.

3 Drain the pasta and return it to the saucepan. Gently mix in the figs, ham and Gorgonzola and transfer to serving plates. Spoon over the dressing and serve.

Tip The success of this recipe depends on really well-flavoured ingredients. The figs must be sweet, ripe and juicy, and the cheese, mature, creamy and salty.

Roast beef linguine with Parmesan dressing

This is a stunning starter for smart entertaining, but don't follow it with anything too heavy! The dressing can be made ahead if you like.

PREPARATION TIME: 12 minutes

COOKING TIME: 20 minutes

SERVES: 6

400 g (13 oz) piece beef fillet

125 ml (4 fl oz) olive oil

2 organic egg yolks

1 tablespoon white wine vinegar

2 tablespoons single cream

1 small garlic clove, crushed

15 g (½ oz) chopped herbs, such as parsley, thyme, chives or mint

50 g (2 oz) Parmesan cheese, grated

300 g (10 oz) fresh linguine

salt and pepper

1 Cut away any pieces of fat from the meat. Pat it dry and put in a small roasting tin. Season with salt and pepper and drizzle with 1 tablespoon oil. Roast in a preheated oven, 220°C (425°F), Gas Mark 7, for 20 minutes.

2 Meanwhile, bring a large saucepan of salted water to the boil, ready to cook the pasta. Put the egg yolks, vinegar and cream in a blender or food processor and blend until smooth. Alternatively, whisk the ingredients together in a bowl. Whisk in all but 1 tablespoon of the remaining oil, then the garlic, herbs and Parmesan.

3 Remove the meat from the oven, transfer it to a chopping board and cover with foil. Reserve any pan juices. Add the pasta to the water, return to the boil and cook for 2 minutes until tender. Drain the pasta, return it to the pan and toss with the remaining oil, the pan juices and about one-third of the sauce.

4 Slice the beef as thinly as possible. Heap the pasta on to warm serving plates and pile the beef on top. Spoon over the remaining sauce and serve.

Stuffed pasta shells
Packed with a buttery crab stuffing, this recipe is delicious but very rich, so serve it as a snack or before a reasonably light main course.

PREPARATION TIME: 25 minutes

COOKING TIME: 25 minutes

SERVES: 4

125 g (4 oz) conchiglie gigante

25 g (1 oz) butter

1 fennel bulb, finely chopped

2 tablespoons chopped tarragon

3 tablespoons chopped parsley

275 g (9 oz) dressed crab

100 g (3½ oz) crème fraîche

2 tablespoons white wine

1 garlic clove, crushed

40 g (1½ oz) breadcrumbs

salt and pepper

1 Bring a large saucepan of salted water to the boil. Add the pasta, return to the boil and cook for 15 minutes until tender. Meanwhile, melt half the butter in a frying pan and fry the fennel until golden. Stir in the herbs, dressed crab and a little pepper.

2 Drain the pasta well. Use a teaspoon to pack the crab mixture into the pasta shells and arrange them in a single layer, filled side up, in a shallow baking dish.

3 Soften the crème fraîche in a small saucepan and stir in the wine. Melt the remaining butter in the frying pan and stir in the garlic and breadcrumbs.

4 Spoon the crème fraîche mixture over the pasta and scatter with the garlic crumbs. Cook under a preheated grill for 3–5 minutes. Spoon on to serving plates and drizzle with the crème fraîche juices.

Smoked salmon ravioli with dill cream sauce

Japanese wasabi paste is a very hot, fragrant horseradish but you can use ordinary horseradish if preferred.

PREPARATION TIME: 50 minutes, plus standing

COOKING TIME: 15 minutes

SERVES: 6

175 g (6 oz) smoked salmon

1½ teaspoons wasabi paste

75 g (3 oz) ricotta cheese

1 quantity pasta dough (see page 8)

150 ml (¼ pint) fish stock

150 ml (¼ pint) white wine

150 ml (¼ pint) double cream

4 tablespoons chopped dill

salt and pepper

1 Finely chop the salmon and place it in a bowl with the wasabi paste and ricotta. Beat well until evenly mixed.

2 Use the pasta dough and smoked salmon mixture to make ravioli, following the method on page 12. Leave to dry for 30 minutes before cooking.

3 Put the fish stock and wine in a saucepan. Bring to the boil and boil rapidly for about 10 minutes or until it has reduced to about 100 ml (3½ fl oz). Meanwhile, bring a large saucepan of salted water to the boil and cook the ravioli in two or three batches for 4–5 minutes (once the water has returned to the boil), until they're just tender.

4 Stir the cream and dill into the reduced stock and heat until bubbling around the edges. Season to taste with salt and pepper. Drain the ravioli and serve in warm shallow dishes with the sauce.

Smoked salmon ravioli with dill cream sauce

Tagliatelle with shaved truffles

Truffles are hugely expensive, particularly the white (alba) ones, and are best served simply shaved over pasta with nothing but the best Parmesan cheese.

PREPARATION TIME: 5 minutes

COOKING TIME: 3 minutes

SERVES: 4

300 g (10 oz) fresh tagliatelle

75 g (3 oz) unsalted butter

40 g (1½ oz) Parmesan cheese, grated

1 small white or black truffle

salt and pepper

1 Bring a large saucepan of salted water to the boil. Add the pasta and cook for 2–3 minutes until just tender. Drain and return to the saucepan.

2 Dot the butter over the pasta and stir in the Parmesan and salt and pepper.

3 Pile the pasta on to warm serving plates. Use a potato peeler or small mandoline slice to shave the truffle over the pasta and serve immediately.

Tip Fresh truffles are available in winter, or you can get them, preserved in tiny jars, throughout the year. A more affordable alternative is to drizzle fresh pasta with truffle oil for a simple starter or snack. A white truffle sauce is also available, and this can be stirred into pasta.

Pasta and asparagus parcels

For the final rolling of the pasta, use a rolling pin rather than a machine. The wafer thin sheets will crumple up as they cook which looks particularly effective.

PREPARATION TIME: 25 minutes, plus drying

COOKING TIME: 15–20 minutes

SERVES: 6

½ **quantity plain or tomato-flavoured pasta dough (see pages 8 and 11)**

flour, for dusting

125 g (4 oz) butter

4 tablespoons chopped fennel

1 small garlic clove, crushed

75 g (3 oz) prosciutto, finely chopped

2 teaspoons white wine vinegar

625 g (1¼ lb) asparagus, trimmed

2 tablespoons sun-dried tomato pesto

salt and pepper

1 Line 2 trays with flour-dusted tea towels or kitchen paper. Cut the pasta into 3 pieces and roll each piece into a long, thin strip (see method on page 9). When the strips are about 50 cm (20 inches) long, cut them in half widthways and roll each piece by hand until wafer thin. Transfer to the lightly floured trays and leave for 30 minutes.

2 Bring a large saucepan of salted water to the boil, ready to cook the pasta. Melt the butter in a small saucepan. Stir in the chopped fennel, garlic, prosciutto, vinegar and a little pepper and cook gently for 1 minute.

3 Put the asparagus in a frying pan. Just cover with boiling water and simmer gently until just tender. Drain and refresh under cold running water. Lower the pasta into the boiling water, return to the boil and cook for 2 minutes. Drain. When it is cool enough to handle, spread each piece with a little pesto, place a bundle of asparagus in the centre and fold the ends of the pasta over the asparagus. Place in a large, shallow dish or baking sheet and cover loosely with foil. Cook in a preheated oven, 190°C (375°F), Gas Mark 5, for 5–10 minutes or until heated through. Meanwhile, warm the butter.

4 Transfer the asparagus parcels to warm serving plates and drizzle with the butter.

Gnocchi with broad beans and Parmesan

This is a potato-based gnocchi, shaped traditionally into grooved nuggets and dressed up with beans and crispy bacon.

PREPARATION TIME: 10 minutes

COOKING TIME: 15 minutes

SERVES: 4–6

1 quantity Gnocchi (see page 15)

50 g (2 oz) butter, plus extra for greasing

200 g (7 oz) baby broad beans

2 tablespoons olive oil

75 g (3 oz) smoked bacon or pancetta, finely chopped

40 g (1½ oz) Parmesan cheese, grated

salt and pepper

1 Make, shape and cook the gnocchi. Once drained, tip them into a shallow, lightly buttered ovenproof dish or 4–6 individual dishes.

2 Blanch the beans in boiling water for 2 minutes. Drain thoroughly and scatter over and around the gnocchi.

3 Melt the butter with the oil in a frying pan and fry the bacon or pancetta until crisp and golden. Spoon over the gnocchi and drizzle over the juices in the pan.

4 Sprinkle with the Parmesan and bake in a preheated oven, 200°C (400°F), Gas Mark 6, for 10–15 minutes until heated through.

Tip If you're making this recipe ahead, assemble the dish, leave to cool, loosely covered with clingfilm, and chill for several hours. Bake as above, allowing a little extra cooking time for the gnocchi to heat through.

Simply sauces *The reason for the infinite variety of different types of fresh and dried pasta is not solely visual. The grooves, curves, pockets and cavities of pasta shapes are designed to trap a sauce so that every mouthful combines the perfect balance of pasta and sauce. There are no hard and fast rules about which pasta should be served with which sauce, although traditionally a bolognese sauce is always served with tagliatelle and a carbonara with spaghetti.*

Generally, creamy sauces and any fairly smooth sauces are best served with long pasta ribbons, such as tagliatelle or linguine, because the sauce easily coats the pasta and can be lifted from the plate without making a mess. Chunkier sauces tend to be served with short pasta shapes so that both pasta and bite-sized sauce ingredients are evenly balanced.

Amatriciana sauce

This is a good choice for those who like their tomato sauce to have a punchier flavour. If the tomatoes are lacking in flavour, stir in a generous dollop of sun-dried tomato paste.

PREPARATION TIME: 15 minutes

COOKING TIME: 40 minutes

SERVES: 4

1 kg (2 lb) ripe, full-flavoured tomatoes
5 tablespoons olive oil
1 large onion, finely chopped
1 celery stick, finely chopped
75 g (3 oz) pancetta, cubed
3 garlic cloves, crushed
1 hot red chilli, deseeded and finely chopped
salt and pepper

1 Put the tomatoes in a heatproof bowl, cover with boiling water and leave for about 2 minutes or until the skins start to split. Pour away the water. Peel and roughly chop the tomatoes.

2 Heat the oil in a large, heavy-based saucepan and gently fry the onion, celery and pancetta, stirring frequently, for 6–8 minutes or until softened. Add the garlic and chilli and fry for a further 2 minutes.

3 Stir in the chopped tomatoes and cook gently, uncovered, stirring frequently, for about 30 minutes or until the sauce is very thick and pulpy. Check the seasoning and serve.

Sausage, chestnut and pickled walnut sauce

Venison, wild boar or any other gamey sausages are ideal for this dish, which makes a comforting and warming winter supper.

PREPARATION TIME: 15 minutes

COOKING TIME: 25 minutes

SERVES: 4

25 g (1 oz) butter

400 g (13 oz) sausages, skinned

1 large onion, finely chopped

1 teaspoon chopped rosemary

200 ml (7 fl oz) red wine

200 g (7 oz) cooked chestnuts, chopped

4 pickled walnuts, chopped, plus
   3 tablespoons vinegar from the jar

4 tablespoons chopped flat leaf parsley

salt and pepper

1 Melt the butter in a large saucepan. Add the skinned sausages, one at a time, mashing them in the pan with a fork to break them into small pieces.

2 Add the onion and fry gently, stirring and continuing to break up the sausages with the edge of a wooden spoon, for about 10 minutes or until browned.

3 Stir in the rosemary and wine and cook gently for 5 minutes.

4 Add the chestnuts, walnuts and the vinegar from the jar. Heat gently for 5 minutes until heated through. Stir in the parsley and season to taste with salt and pepper.

Jerusalem artichoke and crispy bacon sauce

The flavour of these artichokes vaguely resembles that of globe artichoke hearts, and they make an equally good partner to pasta.

PREPARATION TIME: 15 minutes

COOKING TIME: 25 minutes

SERVES: 4

400 g (13 oz) Jerusalem artichokes

25 g (1 oz) butter

150 g (5 oz) streaky bacon, chopped

1 onion, finely chopped

1 celery stick, chopped

¼ teaspoon cayenne pepper

150 ml (¼ pint) chicken or vegetable stock

3 tablespoons double cream

3 tablespoons chopped chives

salt and pepper

1 Cook the artichokes in boiling water for 8–10 minutes until just tender (see tip). Cut into thin slices.

2 Melt half the butter in a saucepan and fry the bacon until it is beginning to colour. Add the onion, celery and cayenne pepper and fry for a further 5 minutes.

3 Stir in the stock and artichokes and bring to the boil. Cover, reduce the heat and simmer gently for 5 minutes.

4 Stir in the cream and chives and season to taste with salt and pepper before serving.

Tip Choose the smoothest artichokes available because the knobblier they are, the more waste there'll be. If they are difficult to peel, cook them in their skins and peel them after cooking.

Spaghetti carbonara

It's the heat from the steaming hot spaghetti that lightly cooks the creamy egg sauce. This is a quickly assembled dish, so have everything ready before you begin.

PREPARATION TIME: 10 minutes

COOKING TIME: 5 minutes

SERVES: 4

4 egg yolks

2 eggs

150 ml (¼ pint) single cream

50 g (2 oz) Parmesan cheese, grated

2 tablespoons olive oil

100 g (3½ oz) pancetta or streaky bacon, finely sliced

2 garlic cloves, crushed

400 g (13 oz) fresh spaghetti

salt and pepper

1 Beat together the egg yolks, whole eggs, cream, Parmesan and plenty of pepper.

2 Heat the oil in a large frying pan and fry the pancetta or bacon for 3–4 minutes or until golden and turning crisp. Add the garlic and cook for a further 1 minute.

3 Meanwhile, bring a large saucepan of salted water to the boil, add the spaghetti and cook for 2 minutes or until tender.

4 Drain the spaghetti and immediately tip it into the frying pan. Turn off the heat and stir in the egg mixture until the eggs are lightly cooked. Serve immediately. (If the heat of the pasta doesn't quite cook the egg sauce, turn on the heat and cook briefly, stirring.)

Spaghetti carbonara

Spicy meatball sauce

This recipe combines chunky, herby meatballs and a tangy, fresh tomato sauce. Well-flavoured tomatoes are essential, but you can use canned tomatoes instead of fresh.

PREPARATION TIME: 25 minutes

COOKING TIME: 25 minutes

SERVES: 4

500 g (1 lb) lean minced lamb

1 large red onion, finely chopped

2 tablespoons finely chopped oregano

50 g (2 oz) breadcrumbs

3 tablespoons olive oil

3 garlic cloves, crushed

500 g (1 lb) tomatoes, skinned and chopped

1 teaspoon caster sugar

1 teaspoon mild chilli powder

finely grated rind of 1 lemon

salt and pepper

1 Put the lamb, onion, oregano, breadcrumbs and a little salt and pepper in a bowl and mix well together. This is most easily done with your hands. Shape the mixture into small balls about 3 cm (1¼ inches) in diameter.

2 Heat the oil in a large frying pan and gently fry the meatballs, shaking the pan frequently, for 8–10 minutes or until they are browned.

3 Remove the meatballs with a slotted spoon and set aside. Then add the garlic, tomatoes, sugar, chilli powder, lemon rind and salt and pepper to the pan. Heat gently, stirring, until the mixture is bubbling.

4 Return the meatballs to the pan, cover with a lid and cook gently for 10 minutes or until the meatballs are cooked through and tender. Serve immediately.

Bolognese sauce

Bolognese, or ragu, *is usually served with tagliatelle rather than spaghetti. It should be thick and pulpy, rather than thin and gravy-like, so it clings to the pasta it's served with.*

PREPARATION TIME: 15 minutes

COOKING TIME: 1 hour

SERVES: 4

15 g (½ oz) butter

3 tablespoons olive oil

1 large onion, finely chopped

1 celery stick, finely chopped

1 carrot, finely chopped

3 garlic cloves, crushed

500 g (1 lb) lean minced beef

150 ml (¼ pint) red wine

2 x 400 g (13 oz) cans chopped tomatoes

2 tablespoons sun-dried tomato paste

3 tablespoons chopped oregano

3 bay leaves

salt and pepper

grated Parmesan cheese, to serve (optional)

1 Melt the butter with the oil in a large, heavy-based saucepan and gently fry the onion for 5 minutes. Add the celery and carrot and fry gently for a further 2 minutes.

2 Stir in the garlic, then add the minced beef. Fry gently, breaking up the meat, until lightly browned.

3 Add the wine and let the mixture bubble until the wine reduces slightly. Stir in the chopped tomatoes, tomato paste, oregano and bay leaves and bring to the boil.

4 Reduce the heat and cook very gently, uncovered, for about 45 minutes or until the sauce is very thick and pulpy. Check the seasoning, and serve with grated Parmesan, if liked.

Tip In Italy a bolognese sauce is tossed with the pasta rather than spooned on top.

Lamb, leek and peppercorn sauce Use good-quality lamb for this rich, creamy sauce so it's not too watery when you fry it off. Serve with a plain or a spinach-flavoured pasta.

PREPARATION TIME: 10 minutes

COOKING TIME: 20 minutes

SERVES: 4

2 leeks

25 g (1 oz) butter

400 g (13 oz) lean minced lamb

2 garlic cloves, crushed

2 teaspoons plain flour

150 ml (¼ pint) lamb, chicken or vegetable stock

2 tablespoons green peppercorns in brine, rinsed and drained

100 ml (3½ fl oz) crème fraîche

plenty of freshly grated nutmeg

salt

1 Trim and chop the leeks. Melt the butter in a large, shallow pan and gently fry the lamb until lightly browned, stirring frequently and breaking up the meat with a wooden spoon. Add the leeks and garlic and fry gently for a further 5 minutes.

2 Stir in the flour, then the stock and peppercorns and bring the mixture to a gentle simmer. Cover with a lid and cook gently for 10 minutes until the lamb is tender.

3 Stir in the crème fraîche, plenty of nutmeg and a little salt to taste. Heat through gently before serving.

Lamb, leek and peppercorn sauce

Chicken and tarragon sauce

Although this sauce is thin in consistency, it's packed with meaty flavour. Toss the sauce with a pasta shape like fusilli to trap all the delicious juices.

PREPARATION TIME: 10 minutes

COOKING TIME: 1¼ hours

SERVES: 4

3 chicken legs

3 carrots, roughly chopped

1 large onion, roughly chopped

2 celery sticks, roughly chopped

2 bay leaves

200 ml (7 fl oz) crème fraîche

3 tablespoons roughly chopped tarragon

salt and pepper

1 Halve the chicken legs through the joints to separate the thighs from the drumsticks and put them in a large saucepan. Scatter the carrots, onion, celery and bay leaves on top and just cover with water. Heat until simmering then reduce the heat to its lowest setting and cook very gently, uncovered, for about 50 minutes or until the chicken pieces are very tender.

2 Lift out the chicken. Strain the stock, discarding the vegetables and bay leaves, and return to the pan. Bring the stock to the boil and boil rapidly until it is reduced to about a ladleful. This will take 15–20 minutes.

3 Once the chicken is cool enough to handle, chop it into small pieces, discarding the skin and bones.

4 Stir the chicken, crème fraîche, tarragon and a little salt and pepper into the reduced stock and heat through gently before serving.

Chicken liver and sage sauce

Chicken livers have a smooth, creamy texture like no other meat. Serve with a tomato salad or plenty of crispy leaves, in a fresh, tangy dressing.

PREPARATION TIME: 10 minutes

COOKING TIME: 10 minutes

SERVES: 3–4

500 g (1 lb) fresh chicken livers

20 sage leaves

3 tablespoons olive oil

25 g (1 oz) butter

2 shallots, finely chopped

2 garlic cloves, crushed

4 tablespoons Marsala

3 tablespoons single cream

salt and pepper

1 Rinse the chicken livers and thoroughly dry on kitchen paper. Cut into small pieces, discarding any white, fatty parts. Reserve 12 of the largest sage leaves and finely shred the remainder.

2 Heat the oil in a large frying pan. Add the whole sage leaves and fry quickly for 30 seconds until crisp. Remove with a slotted spoon and pat dry on kitchen paper to remove the excess oil.

3 Add the butter to the pan and fry the shallots for 3 minutes until softened. Stir in the garlic, chicken livers and salt and pepper and fry gently, stirring, for a further 2–3 minutes or until the livers are lightly browned but still slightly pink in the centre.

4 Stir in the Marsala, cream and shredded sage leaves and heat through gently until bubbling. Serve scattered with the fried sage leaves.

Tip This sauce is particularly good with herb- or black pepper-flavoured fresh tagliatelle.

Game and mushroom sauce

Pasta sauces range from delicate to intensely rich and meaty. This is definitely one of the latter, a wintry comfort food that combines delicious seasonal ingredients.

PREPARATION TIME: 15 minutes

COOKING TIME: 20 minutes

SERVES: 4

200 g (7 oz) lean pork, roughly chopped

4 pigeon breasts, roughly chopped

8 juniper berries

25 g (1 oz) butter

1 onion, chopped

2 garlic cloves, crushed

2 bay leaves

several sprigs of thyme

250 g (8 oz) mixed wild mushrooms, such as girolles, chanterelles or ceps, sliced if large

150 ml (¼ pint) rich chicken stock

100 ml (3½ fl oz) double cream

2 tablespoons chopped parsley

salt and pepper

1 Blitz the pork in a food processor until chopped into very small pieces. Remove from the processor. Add the pigeon breasts to the processor and whiz until finely chopped.

2 Use a pestle and mortar to crush the juniper berries. Melt the butter in a large frying pan, add the pork, pigeon breasts and onion and fry gently, stirring frequently, until pale golden. Add the garlic, bay leaves, thyme and juniper and cook gently for a further 5 minutes.

3 Add the mushrooms and continue cooking for about 5 minutes or until the moisture from the mushrooms has evaporated.

4 Stir in the stock and cream and heat until bubbling. Cook for about 3 minutes until heated through. Stir in the parsley, season to taste and serve.

Smoked salmon, ginger and lime butter

Savoury butters are utterly delicious when they melt into hot food, and this aromatic salmon butter for pasta is no exception.

PREPARATION TIME: 10 minutes

SERVES: 4

100 g (3½ oz) smoked salmon

100 g (3½ oz) unsalted butter, softened

25 g (1 oz) fresh root ginger, peeled and grated

finely grated rind of 1 lime, plus 1 tablespoon juice

2 tablespoons finely chopped parsley or chervil

plenty of black pepper

1 Chop the smoked salmon into small pieces and put them in a bowl with the butter, ginger, lime rind and juice, parsley or chervil and plenty of pepper. Beat well until evenly combined.

2 Tip into a small bowl, cover and chill for up to 3 days until ready to use.

Tip Once you've melted this butter over freshly cooked, hot pasta, pile it on to serving plates and serve with extra lime wedges for squeezing over.

Variations Use the same quantity of cooked prawns or white crab meat instead of the salmon. Other aromatic ingredients, such as garlic, herbs, horseradish and capers, also make lovely additions to flavoured butters for dressing pasta.

Squid and tomato tartare

This colourful, fresh, tangy sauce has a distinctly Mediterranean flavour and is perfect with almost any pasta. It looks stunning with squid ink pasta.

PREPARATION TIME: 10 minutes

COOKING TIME: 10 minutes

SERVES: 2–3

300 g (10 oz) small squid

3 tablespoons olive oil

2 garlic cloves, crushed

400 g (13 oz) can chopped tomatoes

2 tablespoons sun-dried tomato paste

4 tablespoons chopped parsley

25 g (1 oz) gherkins, finely chopped

2 tablespoons capers in brine, drained, rinsed and chopped

salt and pepper

1 Rinse the squid and thinly slice into rings. Thoroughly pat them dry on kitchen paper. (If the tentacles are present, cut these from the heads and use as well.)

2 Heat the oil in a frying pan and gently fry the squid for 2–3 minutes or until puffed into rings. Add the garlic and fry gently for 1 minute.

3 Add the tomatoes, tomato paste, parsley, gherkins and capers to the pan. Simmer gently for 5 minutes or until the sauce is thickened and heated through. Season to taste with salt and pepper and serve.

Monkfish, saffron and mascarpone sauce

Monkfish is great for tossing with pasta because it holds its shape well. This rich, creamy sauce is particularly good with fresh pasta.

PREPARATION TIME: 10 minutes

COOKING TIME: 15 minutes

SERVES: 3–4

½ teaspoon saffron threads

350 g (11½ oz) monkfish fillet

25 g (1 oz) butter

1 fennel bulb, finely chopped

1 teaspoon fennel seeds, crushed

250 g (8 oz) mascarpone cheese

splash of white wine

salt and pepper

1 Crumble the saffron threads into 2 tablespoons just-boiled water in a small dish and leave to stand while you prepare the sauce.

2 Pat the fish dry on kitchen paper and cut away any bone and dark areas of the flesh. Thinly slice the fish and season lightly with salt and pepper.

3 Melt the butter in a frying pan and gently fry the monkfish for 2 minutes or until it is opaque. Lift out with a slotted spoon and add the fennel and seeds to the pan. Fry gently for 5 minutes or until softened.

4 Add the mascarpone to the pan with the saffron, the soaking liquid and wine and cook, stirring, until the cheese is melted and bubbling. Stir in the monkfish and cook gently for 2–3 minutes until cooked through. Check the seasoning and serve.

Monkfish, saffron and mascarpone sauce

Crayfish sauce with tarragon *Curly pink crayfish tails, cooked and brined, are often available from the fishmonger or in little tubs from the supermarket.*

PREPARATION TIME: 10 minutes

COOKING TIME: 20 minutes

SERVES: 2–4

300 ml (½ pint) homemade or bought fresh fish stock (see tip)

½ glass of white wine

1 bay leaf

several sprigs of thyme

15 g (½ oz) butter

1 tablespoon plain flour

150 ml (¼ pint) double cream

1 tablespoon tomato paste

1 tablespoon chopped tarragon

1 tablespoon brandy (optional)

150 g (5 oz) crayfish tails, thoroughly rinsed and drained

salt and pepper

1 Put the stock, wine and herbs in a saucepan and bring to the boil. Boil until reduced to about 200 ml (7 fl oz). This will take 10–15 minutes.

2 Melt the butter in a separate saucepan. Add the flour and cook for 1 minute to make a golden paste. Gradually blend in the stock, discarding the herbs. Cook gently, stirring until thickened and smooth.

3 Stir in the cream, tomato paste, tarragon and brandy, if using, and heat gently until simmering.

4 Stir in the crayfish tails and heat through gently for 2 minutes. Check the seasoning and serve.

Tip A simple fish stock is easy to make from leftover raw white fish bones and trimmings. Put the pieces in a pan with a small chopped onion, a bay leaf, a teaspoon of peppercorns, a chopped celery stick and several lemon slices. Simmer gently for 40 minutes then strain. Chill overnight or freeze until required.

Chunky tapenade

This is a variation on a traditional tapenade, with the addition of hot chilli and spices, coarsely blended to make a textured pasta sauce.

PREPARATION TIME: 5 minutes

COOKING TIME: 2 minutes

SERVES: 4

1 teaspoon crushed cumin seeds

1 teaspoon crushed coriander seeds

150 g (5 oz) pitted black olives

25 g (1 oz) capers, drained and rinsed

½ 50 g (2 oz) can anchovy fillets in olive oil

1 garlic clove, chopped

small handful of flat leaf parsley

15 g (½ oz) red jalapeño chillies in sweet vinegar, drained

125 ml (4 fl oz) olive oil

1 Gently heat the cumin and coriander seeds in a small dry frying pan until they start to toast.

2 Tip the seeds into a food processor and add the olives, capers, anchovy fillets and their oil, garlic, parsley and chillies.

3 Blend lightly, until the ingredients start to mix together.

4 Add the oil and blend briefly to a chunky paste. Transfer the sauce to a small bowl and cover until needed.

Tip If you toss this sauce with very hot, steaming pasta you won't need to heat it through first. To make it really hot you might prefer to heat it gently in a small pan for a couple of minutes before tossing it with the pasta.

Vongole sauce

Small clams, served in a rich tomato sauce and tossed with pasta, make up the classic southern Italian dish, spaghetti vongole. Use linguine or fresh or dried spaghetti.

PREPARATION TIME: 20 minutes

COOKING TIME: 20 minutes

SERVES: 4

1 kg (2 lb) small fresh clams
150 ml (¼ pint) dry white wine
4 tablespoons olive oil
1 small onion, finely chopped
3 garlic cloves, crushed
2 x 400 g (13 oz) cans chopped tomatoes
1 teaspoon caster sugar
2 bay leaves
small handful of flat leaf parsley, chopped
finely grated rind and juice of ½ lemon
salt and pepper

1 Scrub the clams, discarding any damaged ones or open ones that do not close when tapped with a knife.

2 Bring the wine to the boil in a large, heavy-based saucepan. Tip in the clams, cover with a tight-fitting lid and cook for 3–4 minutes, shaking the pan frequently until the shells have opened. Remove the clams, reserving the liquor, and shell about half of them, discarding any that remain closed.

3 Heat the oil in the cleaned pan. Add the onion and cook gently for 5 minutes. Add the garlic and cook for a further 1 minute. Add the tomatoes, sugar, bay leaves and the reserved clam liquor and bring to the boil. Reduce the heat and simmer gently for about 10 minutes until the sauce is thickened and pulpy.

4 Stir in the clams, parsley and lemon rind and juice. Heat through for 1 minute. Check the seasoning and serve.

Béchamel sauce

This creamy white sauce is used as a topping for lasagne and other pasta bakes. If there's additional cream in the pasta recipe you might prefer to use extra milk instead.

PREPARATION TIME: 10 minutes

COOKING TIME: 5 minutes

MAKES: 600 ml (1 pint)

50 g (2 oz) butter

40 g (1½ oz) plain flour

300 ml (½ pint) milk

300 ml (½ pint) single cream or use 600 ml (1 pint) milk and omit the cream

freshly grated nutmeg

salt and pepper

1 Melt the butter in a heavy-based saucepan. Stir in the flour and cook gently for 1 minute, stirring to make a smooth paste.

2 Remove the pan from the heat and gradually add the milk, beating well with a wooden spoon. If the mixture becomes lumpy, beat it briefly with a balloon whisk.

3 Stir in the cream, a little nutmeg and salt and pepper and return the pan to the heat. Cook gently, stirring well, until the sauce is smooth and thickened.

Three cheese sauce
When mixing several cheeses in a dish it's best to use ones with strongly contrasting flavours and textures, such as provolone or fontina, ricotta, and Parmesan or pecorino.

PREPARATION TIME: 5 minutes

COOKING TIME: 5 minutes

SERVES: 2

4 tablespoons lemon-infused olive oil

3 tablespoons chopped chives

1 teaspoon finely chopped rosemary

good pinch of cayenne pepper

150 g (5 oz) ricotta cheese

50 g (2 oz) provolone or fontina cheese, thinly sliced

50 g (2 oz) Parmesan or pecorino cheese, grated

1 Put the oil, chives, rosemary and cayenne pepper in a saucepan and heat gently for a couple of minutes so that the herbs and spice infuse the oil.

2 Stir in the ricotta and heat gently, stirring, until it has softened.

3 Stir in the remaining cheeses and heat through gently for 1 minute until the sauce is smooth and creamy. Serve immediately.

Fresh tomato sauce

The rich, fruity flavour of this sauce is one of the best and most useful in pasta dishes. Use it as it is or add other ingredients, such as capers, anchovies, pancetta or torn basil.

PREPARATION TIME: 15 minutes

COOKING TIME: 30 minutes

MAKES: 750 ml (1¼ pints), enough for 4 servings

1 kg (2 lb) very ripe, full-flavoured tomatoes
100 ml (3½ fl oz) olive oil
1 onion, finely chopped
2 garlic cloves, crushed
2 tablespoons chopped oregano
sprinkling of caster sugar
salt and pepper

1 Put the tomatoes in a heatproof bowl, cover with boiling water and leave for about 2 minutes or until the skins start to split. Pour away the water. Peel and roughly chop the tomatoes.

2 Heat the oil in a large, heavy-based saucepan and gently fry the onion for 5 minutes or until softened but not browned. Add the garlic and fry for a further 1 minute.

3 Add the tomatoes and cook, stirring frequently, for 20–25 minutes or until the sauce is thickened and pulpy.

4 Stir in the oregano and season to taste with salt and pepper. If the sauce is very sharp, add a sprinkling of caster sugar.

Tip This is a good sauce to make in large quantities if you have a glut of home-grown tomatoes or a supply from a farmers' market. Freeze in small bags.

Variation Canned tomatoes make a good alternative if the only fresh ones available don't look very appetizing. Substitute two 400 g (13 oz) cans of chopped tomatoes and cook until pulpy.

Green pepper and coriander pesto

This richly flavoured sauce makes a lovely alternative to a traditional pesto (see variation). Toss with freshly cooked pasta or use as a pasta filling.

PREPARATION TIME: 10 minutes

COOKING TIME: 15 minutes

MAKES: 400 g (13 oz), enough for 4 generous servings

- 100 ml (3½ fl oz) extra virgin olive oil
- 2 green peppers, deseeded and roughly chopped
- 1 teaspoon caster sugar
- 75 g (3 oz) pine nuts
- 75 g (3 oz) Parmesan cheese, roughly sliced
- 2 garlic cloves, crushed
- 40 g (1½ oz) coriander leaves
- 15 g (½ oz) flat leaf parsley
- 1 tablespoon lemon juice
- salt and pepper

1 Heat 3 tablespoons oil in a frying pan and fry the peppers gently for 10–15 minutes until just beginning to colour. Stir in the sugar.

2 Tip into a food processor with the pine nuts, Parmesan, garlic, coriander and parsley. Process lightly to a very coarse paste, scraping the mixture down from the sides of the bowl if necessary.

3 Add the remaining olive oil, lemon juice and a little salt and pepper and blend again to a thick paste. Cover and chill for up to 3 days.

Variation To make a Basil and Pine Nut Pesto, blend 75 g (3 oz) pine nuts, 75 g (3 oz) sliced Parmesan, 2 garlic cloves and 50 g (2 oz) basil leaves in a food processor to make a thick paste. Add 100 ml (3½ fl oz) olive oil, salt and pepper and blend.

Sun-dried tomato and almond pesto *If you use sun-dried tomatoes in oil, drain them first (there's no need to soak them) and substitute their oil for the olive oil.*

PREPARATION TIME: 10 minutes, plus soaking

COOKING TIME: 5 minutes

SERVES: 4

100 g (3½ oz) sun-dried tomatoes

75 g (3 oz) blanched almonds, roughly chopped

2 garlic cloves, roughly chopped

150 ml (¼ pint) olive oil

25 g (1 oz) Parmesan cheese, roughly sliced

salt and pepper

1 Put the tomatoes in a bowl, cover with boiling water and leave to soak for 30 minutes until softened. Put the almonds in a dry frying pan and heat very gently, shaking the pan frequently until the almonds are beginning to turn pale golden in colour.

2 Blitz the almonds in a food processor until finely chopped. Thoroughly drain the tomatoes and add to the food processor with the garlic, half the oil and the Parmesan.

3 Blend to a thick paste, scraping the mixture down from the sides of the bowl. Add the remaining oil and blend until smooth. Season to taste with salt and pepper. This sauce can be stored in the refrigerator, covered, for up to 3–4 days.

Roasted vegetable sauce

This sauce is blended before roasting so the vegetables roast to an appetizing crispiness. It's perfect with a fresh ribbon pasta such as tagliatelle or pappardelle.

PREPARATION TIME: 10 minutes

COOKING TIME: 1 hour

SERVES: 4

500 g (1 lb) aubergines, roughly chopped

300 g (10 oz) courgettes, roughly chopped

3 red peppers, deseeded and cut into chunks

2 red onions, chopped

2 teaspoons chopped rosemary

125 ml (4 fl oz) extra virgin olive oil

1 tablespoon balsamic vinegar

1 tablespoon clear honey

salt and pepper

1 Whiz the aubergines in a food processor until chopped into small, uneven pieces and tip into a large roasting tin. Whiz the courgettes and peppers and add to the tin. Stir in the onions and rosemary and drizzle with 100 ml (3½ fl oz) oil.

2 Roast the vegetables in a preheated oven, 200°C (400°F), Gas Mark 6, for about 1 hour, turning them frequently until they are deep golden and beginning to caramelize.

3 Blend the remaining oil with the balsamic vinegar and honey. Drizzle over the vegetables, season lightly and mix well.

Tip This sauce goes really well with a sprinkling of a contrastingly salty cheese such as Parmesan, pecorino or grana padano.

Roast garlic, spinach and mushroom sauce

This is a deliciously indulgent, creamy sauce. Although a whole head of garlic is used, it's roasted first, giving a mellow, smooth flavour.

PREPARATION TIME: 10 minutes

COOKING TIME: 50 minutes

SERVES: 4

1 small head of garlic

1 tablespoon olive oil

200 g (7 oz) chestnut mushrooms, thinly sliced

200 g (7 oz) baby spinach leaves

200 g (7 oz) cream cheese

plenty of freshly grated nutmeg

100 ml (3½ fl oz) single cream

salt and pepper

1 Nestle the whole garlic in a little foil and roast in a preheated oven, 200°C (400°F), Gas Mark 6, for about 35–45 minutes until it is tender when pierced with a knife.

2 Meanwhile, heat the oil in a large saucepan and gently fry the mushrooms until they are beginning to brown. Add the spinach, cover with a lid and heat gently for a couple of minutes until the spinach has wilted.

3 Remove the roasted garlic from the oven, leave to cool slightly, then slice off the base and squeeze out the contents of each clove. Put them in a food processor with the cream cheese and plenty of nutmeg and blend until smooth.

4 Turn the garlic mixture into a small saucepan, add the cream and heat gently, stirring with a wooden spoon, to make a smooth sauce.

5 Add the mushroom and spinach mixture and heat through. Check the seasoning and serve.

Roast garlic, spinach and mushroom sauce

Sweet potato and chickpea sauce

This recipe provides an interesting contrast between the savouriness of the spicy potatoes and bursts of sweetness from the raisins.

PREPARATION TIME: 15 minutes

COOKING TIME: 25 minutes

SERVES: 4

4 tablespoons olive oil

2 tablespoons flaked almonds

1 large onion, chopped

3 garlic cloves, crushed

½ teaspoon ground cinnamon

½ teaspoon crushed dried chillies

good pinch of ground turmeric

500 g (1 lb) sweet potatoes, cut into 1 cm (½ inch) dice

450 ml (¾ pint) vegetable stock

400 g (13 oz) can chickpeas, drained and rinsed

15 g (½ oz) raisins

salt and pepper

1 Heat the oil in a saucepan and fry the almonds until lightly browned. Lift out with a slotted spoon. Add the onion to the pan and gently fry for 5 minutes or until softened. Add the garlic and spices and fry for a further 1 minute. Add the sweet potatoes and fry for a further 5 minutes.

2 Stir in the stock and chickpeas and bring to the boil. Reduce the heat and simmer gently, covered, for about 10 minutes or until the sauce is pulpy and the sweet potatoes are tender. Use a potato masher to break up the sweet potatoes without mashing them to a pulp.

3 Stir the raisins and almonds into the sauce, then season to taste before serving.

Walnut sauce

This is a really useful storecupboard pasta sauce, though do make sure that the walnuts still taste fresh because they quickly go stale, particularly if the pack is open.

PREPARATION TIME: 10 minutes, plus soaking

COOKING TIME: 5 minutes

SERVES: 4

2 slices white bread, about 75 g (3 oz) in total

250 ml (8 fl oz) milk

250 g (8 oz) shelled walnuts

2 garlic cloves, chopped

100 ml (3½ fl oz) mild olive oil

50 g (2 oz) grated Parmesan

6 tablespoons chopped flat leaf parsley

salt and pepper

1 Break the bread into pieces and put them in a small bowl. Add the milk and leave the bread to soak for 10 minutes or until it has absorbed the milk.

2 Lightly toast the walnuts by heating them gently in a large dry frying pan or under a moderate grill.

3 Tip the walnuts into a food processor and add the soaked bread with any unabsorbed milk, the garlic and oil. Blend until smooth, scraping down any chunky pieces from around the sides of the bowl.

4 Add the Parmesan and blend again until smooth. Add the parsley and season to taste with salt and pepper before serving.

Lemon and vodka sauce

This spicy sauce, enlivened with chilli and vodka, might be the answer when you fancy a quick and easy lunch or supper to perk up jaded tastebuds.

PREPARATION TIME: 10 minutes

COOKING TIME: 5 minutes

SERVES: 2

1 lemon

2 tablespoons mild olive oil

2 garlic cloves, thinly sliced

1 red chilli, deseeded and thinly sliced

2 teaspoons chopped thyme, plus a little extra for garnishing

100 g (3½ oz) cream cheese

2 tablespoons vodka

2 tablespoons toasted flaked almonds

salt

1 Pare thin strips of rind from the lemon using a lemon zester. Squeeze 1 tablespoon lemon juice.

2 Heat the oil in a saucepan and add the lemon rind, garlic, chilli and thyme. Fry gently for 2–3 minutes or until the ingredients start to colour.

3 Add the cream cheese to the saucepan and heat through until it softens to the consistency of pouring cream. Stir in the vodka, lemon juice and a little salt.

4 Toss the sauce with the chosen pasta and serve scattered with the toasted almonds and remaining thyme.

Tip This sauce is really good served with fresh linguine or vermicelli.

Meat *In general, smaller quantities of meat are used for pasta dishes than for other main meals, making them a perfect way of stretching good-quality meats to serve several people. The recipes in this chapter range from family meals such as Lasagne to more unusual ideas such as Beetroot Tagliatelle with Roast Duck for a pretty impressive entertaining dish. There are also several pasta bakes, which are so convenient for making ahead and popping in the oven when everyone's hungry. These freeze well so you could double up on the ingredients and freeze half for another time.*

Meat-stuffed pastas are a bit more fiddly to prepare but they can be made and shaped several hours ahead. For longer storage, layer the stuffed shapes in a ridged container, interleaving them with clingfilm. They can be frozen for up to a month.

Spicy sausage bake

Make this quick and easy supper dish with the most garlicky, spicy sausages you can find. Their flavour will mingle with all the other ingredients as they cook.

PREPARATION TIME: 15 minutes

COOKING TIME: 45 minutes

SERVES: 4

450 g (14¹/₂ oz) Italian sausages

2 tablespoons olive oil

1 large red onion, sliced

2 x 400 g (13 oz) cans chopped tomatoes

2 tablespoons chopped oregano

400 g (13 oz) can red kidney beans, drained and rinsed

200 g (7 oz) dried fusilli

175 g (6 oz) fontina cheese, grated

salt and pepper

1 Slice each sausage into quarters. Heat the oil in a large, heavy-based frying pan and gently fry the sausages and onion for about 10 minutes until golden, gently shaking the pan frequently.

2 Add the tomatoes, oregano and red kidney beans. Reduce the heat to its lowest setting and cook gently for 10 minutes.

3 Meanwhile, cook the pasta in plenty of boiling, salted water for about 10 minutes or until just tender. Drain and tip into the frying pan. Add half the fontina and toss the ingredients together until mixed.

4 Tip into a 1.5 litre (2¹/₂ pint) shallow ovenproof dish and scatter with the remaining fontina. Bake in a preheated oven, 200°C (400°F), Gas Mark 6, for 20–25 minutes or until the cheese is melting and golden.

Lasagne

In Italy lasagne is always made with fresh pasta sheets. The availability of dried pasta that needs no precooking gives us the option of being a little lazier about making this wonderful dish.

PREPARATION TIME: 15 minutes

COOKING TIME: 55 minutes

SERVES: 4–5

200 g (7 oz) chicken livers

25 g (1 oz) butter

1 quantity Bolognese Sauce (see page 49)

1 quantity Béchamel Sauce (see page 64)

75 g (3 oz) Parmesan cheese, grated

150 g (5 oz) fresh or dried plain or spinach-flavoured lasagne

freshly grated nutmeg

salt and pepper

1 Bring a large saucepan of salted water to the boil, ready to cook the pasta if using fresh. Rinse the chicken livers, pat them dry on kitchen paper and finely chop, discarding any fatty, white parts. Melt the butter in a small frying pan. Add the livers and a little salt and pepper and fry gently for 5 minutes. Stir into the bolognese sauce.

2 Heat the béchamel sauce in a small saucepan with all but 3 tablespoons of the Parmesan until smooth. Lower the fresh pasta sheets, if using, into the boiling water and return to the boil. Cook for 2 minutes and drain.

3 Spread a quarter of the meat sauce in a thin layer in a shallow, 1.5 litre (2¹/₂ pint) ovenproof dish. Spoon over a quarter of the béchamel sauce and spread the sauce over the meat with the back of a spoon. Arrange one-third of the pasta sheets over the sauce, trimming them to fit around the edges.

4 Repeat the layering of meat sauce, béchamel sauce and pasta into the dish, finishing with a layer of béchamel sauce. Sprinkle with the remaining Parmesan and plenty of freshly grated nutmeg. Bake in a preheated oven, 180°C (350°F), Gas Mark 4, for 40–45 minutes until golden. Leave to stand for 10 minutes before serving.

Macaroni, beef and fennel bake

This is basically a macaroni cheese for meat lovers. Use good-quality, lean minced beef so it's tender and cooks quickly before baking in its creamy sauce.

PREPARATION TIME: 20 minutes

COOKING TIME: 1 hour

SERVES: 4

15 g (½ oz) butter

2 large fennel bulbs, finely chopped

400 g (13 oz) minced beef

2 teaspoons fennel seeds

200 g (7 oz) macaroni

1 quantity Béchamel Sauce (see page 64)

150 ml (¼ pint) single cream

150 g (5 oz) taleggio cheese, thinly sliced

salt and pepper

1 Bring a large saucepan of salted water to the boil, ready to cook the pasta. Melt the butter in a large frying pan and gently fry the fennel for 6–8 minutes or until pale golden. Add the beef and fennel seeds and fry gently for a further 10 minutes, breaking up the meat with a wooden spoon, until browned.

2 Meanwhile, put the macaroni in the water, return it to the boil and cook for 10 minutes or until just tender. Drain and return to the saucepan.

3 Tip the beef and fennel mixture into the saucepan with half the béchamel sauce and the cream and stir together until the pasta and meat are evenly coated.

4 Turn the macaroni mixture into a 1.8 litre (3 pint) ovenproof dish and spread it in an even layer. Spoon the remaining sauce over the top. Arrange the taleggio slices over the sauce and season with salt and pepper. Bake in a preheated oven, 190°C (375°F), Gas Mark 5, for about 40 minutes until pale golden.

Beetroot tagliatelle with roast duck *Like most*
flavoured pastas, beetroot imparts a very subtle flavour to a dish,
and its vivid colour looks fabulous against the other ingredients.

PREPARATION TIME: 20 minutes

COOKING TIME: 40 minutes

SERVES: 4

400 g (13 oz) small red onions

3 tablespoons olive oil

4 small duck breasts

1 tablespoon finely chopped thyme

1 quantity beetroot tagliatelle (see page 11)

200 g (7 oz) sugar snap peas

5 tablespoons balsamic vinegar

50 g (2 oz) butter

2 teaspoons finely chopped mint

salt and pepper

1 Cut the onions into wedges, keeping them intact at the root ends, and scatter them in a roasting tin. Drizzle with 2 tablespoons oil and roast in a preheated oven, 220°C (425°F), Gas Mark 7, for 20 minutes or until beginning to colour. Add the duck to the pan, skin side up. Scatter with the thyme and salt and pepper and roast for a further 15 minutes.

2 Bring a large saucepan of salted water to the boil, ready to cook the pasta. Shred the sugar snap peas lengthways and blanch them in a small pan of boiling water for 1 minute. Remove to a heatproof dish and keep warm.

3 Transfer the onions and duck breasts to the dish of peas and pour the vinegar into the tin, add the butter and 2 tablespoons water. Heat gently until bubbling.

4 Put the pasta in the water, return to the boil and cook for 2 minutes until tender. Drain and return to the pan. Thinly slice the duck and add to the pan with the onions, mint and peas. Toss well together. Spoon on to warm serving plates and drizzle with the balsamic butter.

Beetroot tagliatelle with roast duck

Buckwheat pasta with steak and peppers

Thinly sliced tender steak, sautéed peppers and a sweet chilli sauce make delicious partners to a well-flavoured pasta, such as buckwheat.

PREPARATION TIME: 15 minutes

COOKING TIME: 30 minutes

SERVES: 4

2 tablespoons groundnut or vegetable oil

1 red pepper, deseeded and cut into chunks

2 orange or yellow peppers, deseeded and cut into chunks

1 large red onion, thinly sliced

3 tablespoons sweet chilli sauce

3 tablespoons tomato paste

25 g (1 oz) fresh root ginger, peeled and grated

3 garlic cloves, sliced

200 g (7 oz) small tomatoes, cut into wedges

350 g (11½ oz) dried buckwheat pasta

750 g (1½ lb) rump or sirloin steak

salt

1 Heat the oil in a large, heavy-based frying pan and gently fry the peppers and onion for 10 minutes or until softened and beginning to brown. Bring a large saucepan of salted water to the boil, ready to cook the pasta.

2 Blend together the chilli sauce, tomato paste, ginger and 4 tablespoons water in a small bowl.

3 Add the garlic and tomatoes to the peppers and cook, stirring, for a further 2 minutes. Remove the ingredients from the pan with a slotted spoon and keep them warm. Tip the pasta into the water, return to the boil and cook for 8–10 minutes until just tender.

4 Add the steak to the frying pan and cook for 3 minutes on each side. (This will give a medium cooked steak, still slightly pink in the centre, so reduce the cooking time for rare or increase it for well done.)

5 Transfer the meat to a board and cut it into thin slices. Drain the pasta and return to the pan with the peppers and chilli sauce mixture. Mix well and transfer to warm serving plates. Pile the steak slices on top to serve.

Lamb tortellini

This stuffed pasta recipe takes a while to prepare but is thoroughly rewarding. The tortellini can be stored in the refrigerator for several hours, so there's little last-minute effort.

PREPARATION TIME: about 1 hour, plus cooling and drying

COOKING TIME: 20 minutes

SERVES: 4

50 g (2 oz) butter

350 g (11½ oz) lean minced lamb

1 teaspoon finely chopped rosemary

1 garlic clove, crushed

good pinch of ground cinnamon

25 g (1 oz) provolone cheese, grated, plus extra to serve

1 quantity pasta dough (see page 8)

flour, for dusting

4 tablespoons olive oil

2 small courgettes, thinly sliced

50 g (2 oz) pine nuts

25 g (1 oz) sultanas

100 g (3½ oz) baby spinach

2 teaspoons lemon juice

salt and pepper

1 Melt 15 g (¹/₂ oz) butter in a frying pan and gently fry the lamb for 5 minutes. Add the rosemary, garlic, cinnamon, salt and pepper and cook gently for 2 minutes. Transfer to a bowl, stir in the provolone and leave to cool.

2 Line 2 trays with flour-dusted tea towels or kitchen paper. Roll the pasta using a machine or by hand, following the method on page 9. Use the cooled filling and rolled pasta to shape tortellini, following the method on page 13. Leave on the floured trays to dry for 30 minutes before cooking.

3 Bring a large saucepan of salted water to the boil, ready to cook the pasta. Melt another 15 g (¹/₂ oz) butter in a frying pan with the oil and gently fry the courgettes until lightly browned. Stir in the pine nuts and cook for 2 minutes. Scatter the sultanas and spinach into the pan, cover and cook for 1 minute until the spinach has wilted. Remove from the heat, add the remaining butter and drizzle with the lemon juice. Cover and leave to stand.

4 Put half the tortellini in the pasta water, return to the boil and cook for 5 minutes. Remove and cook the remainder. Toss with the spinach mixture and pile on to warm serving plates. Scatter with extra cheese and serve.

Chicken, mushroom and pasta frittata

This creamy, cheesy dish is rather like a deep, baked omelette, ideal for cutting into wedges and serving with salad.

PREPARATION TIME: 20 minutes

COOKING TIME: 40 minutes

SERVES: 4

150 g (5 oz) dried pappardelle or other wide ribbon noodles

2 skinned chicken breasts, about 300 g (10 oz) in total, thinly sliced

25 g (1 oz) butter

1 tablespoon olive oil

200 g (7 oz) chestnut mushrooms, sliced

6 eggs

150 ml (¼ pint) double cream

75 g (3 oz) Parmesan cheese, grated

3 tablespoons chopped tarragon

2 tablespoons chopped parsley

salt and pepper

1 Bring a large saucepan of salted water to the boil. Add the pasta, return to the boil and cook for 6–8 minutes or until just tender. Drain and return to the pan.

2 Meanwhile, season the chicken lightly. Melt the butter with the oil in a heavy-based frying pan and gently fry the chicken for 5 minutes or until cooked through. Remove with a slotted spoon and add the mushrooms to the pan. Fry for 5 minutes or until the moisture has evaporated.

3 Beat together the eggs, cream and half the Parmesan. Toss the pasta with the chicken, mushrooms and herbs and pile into a frying pan with an ovenproof handle. Pour over the egg mixture and heat gently for a couple of minutes until it starts to set. Sprinkle with the remaining Parmesan and transfer to a preheated oven, 180°C (350°F), Gas Mark 4, for 15–20 minutes or until lightly set.

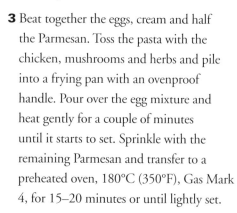

4 Remove the frittata from the oven and allow it to cool slightly before serving.

Chicken, mushroom and pasta frittata

Chicken and basil ravioli

This lovely combination of colours and flavours is perfect for a light meal or a six-portion starter. Save yourself time by reserving the chicken from a roast dinner.

PREPARATION TIME: 45 minutes, plus drying

COOKING TIME: 10 minutes

SERVES: 4

200 g (7 oz) lean cooked chicken, roughly chopped

1 red chilli, deseeded and roughly chopped

50 g (2 oz) basil leaves

3 tablespoons single cream

1 quantity plain or tomato-flavoured pasta (see pages 8 and 11)

flour, for dusting

50 g (2 oz) sun-dried tomatoes in olive oil, drained and finely shredded

75 g (3 oz) butter

salt

plenty of basil leaves, to garnish

1 Put the chicken, chilli, basil leaves and cream in a food processor with a little salt and blend briefly to make a coarse paste.

2 Line 2 trays with flour-dusted tea towels or kitchen paper. Roll the pasta using a machine or by hand, following the method on page 9. Use the chicken mixture and rolled pasta to make ravioli, following the method on page 12. Leave on the floured trays to dry for 30 minutes before cooking.

3 Bring a large saucepan of salted water to the boil, ready to cook the pasta. Melt the butter in a small frying pan until bubbling. As soon as the butter starts to colour, stir in the tomatoes and remove from the heat.

4 Put half the ravioli in the water, return to the boil and cook for 5 minutes. Remove with a slotted spoon and cook the remainder. Pile on to warm serving plates. Spoon over the tomato butter and serve scattered with plenty of basil leaves.

Rabbit sauce with tomatoes and olives *Rabbit is popular in several Mediterranean countries and tastes delicious with herby and tomato sauces.*

PREPARATION TIME: 20 minutes

COOKING TIME: 50 minutes

SERVES: 4

400 g (13 oz) lean rabbit portions

4 tablespoons olive oil

1 small fennel bulb, chopped

2 garlic cloves, crushed

400 g (13 oz) can chopped tomatoes

2 tablespoons chopped oregano

1 glass of white wine

2 tablespoons sun-dried tomato paste

50 g (2 oz) pitted green olives

salt and pepper

1 Cut the rabbit into small pieces, discarding any bones. Season the pieces with salt and pepper. Heat the olive oil in a heavy-based frying pan and gently fry the rabbit, stirring, until pale golden. Remove the rabbit with a slotted spoon.

2 Add the fennel to the pan and fry for 3 minutes or until softened. Stir in the garlic and fry for a 1 further minute.

3 Return the rabbit to the pan with the tomatoes, oregano, wine and tomato paste. Bring to the boil, reduce the heat, cover and simmer gently for 40 minutes until the rabbit is tender.

4 Stir in the olives and season to taste with salt and pepper before serving.

Fettuccine with veal and artichokes

Fresh baby artichokes can be used, if available. Trim the stalks, then simmer in water with a drizzle of lemon juice until tender. Drain and quarter.

PREPARATION TIME: 25 minutes

COOKING TIME: 15 minutes

SERVES: 4

350 g (11½ oz) veal escalopes, cut into 3.5 cm (1½ inch) pieces

75 g (3 oz) butter

300 g (10 oz) jar artichokes in olive oil, drained

300 g (10 oz) plain or spinach-flavoured fresh or dried fettucine (see page 11)

finely grated rind of 1 lemon and 2 tablespoons juice

3 tablespoons roughly chopped tarragon

3 tablespoons salted capers

75 g (3 oz) Gruyère cheese, grated

salt and pepper

1 Season the veal with salt and pepper. Space the pieces slightly apart between sheets of clingfilm and beat with a rolling pin to flatten.

2 Bring a large saucepan of salted water to the boil, ready to cook the pasta. Melt 25 g (1 oz) butter in a large, heavy-based frying pan. Add half the veal pieces and fry quickly for 2 minutes on each side until golden. Remove with a slotted spoon and fry the remainder. Transfer to a plate and keep warm.

3 Fry the artichokes in the pan until beginning to colour. Remove with a slotted spoon. Add the pasta to the boiling water, return to the boil and cook, allowing 2–3 minutes for fresh pasta and 8–10 minutes for dried. Drain and return to the saucepan.

4 Add the remaining butter to the pasta with the lemon rind, juice, tarragon, capers, Gruyére and salt and pepper and toss together. Add the veal, artichokes and any cooking juices and mix gently together. Pile on to warm serving plates.

Fettuccine with veal and artichokes

Fish *Some of the most visually stunning pasta dishes are made with fish, making an impressive choice for entertaining. Meaty fish, such as swordfish and tuna, firm white fish and almost any shellfish team perfectly with pasta, particularly when they're combined with ingredients such as herbs, cream, butter and tomatoes.*

Fish recipes are often served with long pasta such as spaghetti and tagliatelle but you can equally well experiment with any other pasta shapes, shells seeming particularly appropriate. Fish cooks really quickly, so if you're using dried pasta get it cooking before you start on the fish, so one isn't waiting for the other. Most fish pasta recipes should be served as soon as they are ready, except for the Salmon and Leek Bake, which can be assembled in advance and cooked shortly before you're ready to eat.

Seared tuna with angel hair pasta

Of all the long pastas, vermicelli has the finest strands and is sometimes referred to as capelli d'angelo (angel hair).

PREPARATION TIME: 10 minutes, plus marinating

COOKING TIME: 10 minutes

SERVES: 4

100 ml (3½ fl oz) olive oil

2 garlic cloves, crushed

finely grated rind and juice of 1 lime

500 g (1 lb) tuna, in one piece

4 tablespoons chopped dill or fennel

2 tablespoons coarse grain mustard

2 teaspoons caster sugar

4 tablespoons single cream

1 bunch of spring onions, sliced

200 g (7 oz) fine vermicelli

salt and pepper

lime wedges, to serve

1 Mix 1 tablespoon oil with the garlic, lime rind and juice and plenty of pepper. Put the tuna in a dish, spoon over the marinade and cover. Chill for 30 minutes.

2 Heat the remaining oil in a frying pan and fry the spring onions for 1 minute. Remove with a slotted spoon. Add the tuna to the pan and fry gently, turning frequently, until deep golden but still pink in the centre. This will take about 10 minutes. (Test by slicing off the end: it should still be pink in the centre.) Meanwhile, bring a large saucepan of salted water to the boil, ready to cook the pasta. Beat 75 ml (3 fl oz) oil with the dill or fennel, mustard, sugar and cream.

3 Tip the pasta into the boiling water and cook for 3 minutes or until tender. Drain and return to the pan. Stir in half the dressing and the spring onions and pile on to warm plates. Thinly slice the tuna and place on top. Spoon over the remaining dressing and serve with lime wedges.

Salmon and leek bake

Rolling the fish filling in lasagne and packing it into a dish makes an innovative pasta bake. The lavish amount of mascarpone makes it quite rich, so it can easily serve six.

PREPARATION TIME: 30 minutes

COOKING TIME: 50 minutes

SERVES: 6

175 g (6 oz) dried lasagne verdi

625 g (1¼ lb) skinned salmon fillet

4 tablespoons milk

500 g (1 lb) leeks

25 g (1 oz) butter, plus extra for greasing

1 tablespoon coarse grain mustard

500 g (1 lb) mascarpone cheese

75 g (3 oz) grana padano or Parmesan cheese, grated

salt and pepper

1 Bring a large saucepan of salted water to the boil. Add the lasagne sheets, return to the boil and cook for about 10 minutes or until tender. Remove the sheets and immerse in cold water while you prepare the fish.

2 Put the salmon fillet in a frying pan with the milk and a little salt and pepper. Cover and cook gently for 10 minutes until the fish is just cooked through. Remove, reserving the cooking juices, and leave to cool.

3 Trim and chop the leeks. Melt the butter in a frying pan and gently fry the leeks for 6–8 minutes until soft but not browned. Stir in the mustard, 325 g (11 oz) mascarpone and half the grated grana padano or Parmesan. Lightly butter a shallow, 1.5 litre (2½ pint) ovenproof dish.

4 Lay the pasta sheets on the work surface and spread them almost to the edges with the leek mixture. Finely flake the fish, discarding any stray bones, and scatter over the leeks. Roll up the lasagne sheets and cut them across into 5 cm (2 inch) slices. Tuck the slices together, cut sides up, in the dish.

5 Beat the remaining mascarpone with the salmon cooking juices in a small pan, until softened. Spoon over the pasta and sprinkle with the remaining grana padano or Parmesan. Bake in a preheated oven, 190°C (375°F), Gas Mark 5, for 20 minutes until pale golden in colour.

Orecchiette with prawns
Orecchiette has a slightly chewy texture that's good with tangy sauces. Ready-cooked prawns can be used instead of fresh; add them at the last minute.

PREPARATION TIME: 15 minutes

COOKING TIME: 15 minutes

SERVES: 4

6 tablespoons lemon-infused olive oil

15 g (½ oz) oregano and flat leaf parsley leaves

250 g (8 oz) dried orecchiette

250 g (8 oz) raw peeled prawns

400 g (13 oz) can chopped tomatoes

2 tablespoons sun-dried tomato paste

250 g (8 oz) ricotta cheese

salt and pepper

1 Heat 4 tablespoons oil in a large frying pan. Add the herb leaves and fry quickly for 20–30 seconds until they crisp up. Remove with a slotted spoon. Bring a large saucepan of water to the boil, add the pasta and cook for about 12 minutes or until just tender.

2 Meanwhile, pat the prawns dry on kitchen paper and put them in the frying pan. Fry gently for about 2 minutes on each side or until pink right through. Transfer to a plate.

3 Add the chopped tomatoes, tomato paste and a little salt and pepper to the frying pan. Bring to the boil and cook gently for a few minutes or until the sauce is thickened and bubbling.

4 Spoon a small ladleful of the pasta cooking water into the tomato sauce. Drain the pasta and return to the saucepan. Stir the prawns and half the fried herbs into the tomato sauce and add to the pasta. Dot with teaspoonfuls of ricotta and pile on to warm serving plates. Serve scattered with the remaining herbs and drizzled with the remaining olive oil.

Squid ink pasta with seared scallops

The rich, ebony tone of squid ink pasta looks stunning against the delicate scallops and vibrant green leaves.

PREPARATION TIME: 15 minutes

COOKING TIME: 15 minutes

SERVES: 4

20 large scallops with roes

6 tablespoons mild olive oil

2 teaspoons clear honey

2 teaspoons Thai fish sauce

1 tablespoon white wine vinegar

2 teaspoons finely grated fresh ginger

1 quantity bought or homemade squid ink-
flavoured tagliatelle (see page 11)

1 tablespoon pumpkin seeds

150 g (5 oz) rocket or watercress

salt and pepper

1 Bring a large saucepan of salted water to the boil, ready to cook the pasta. Clean the scallops and pat them dry on kitchen paper. Season with salt and pepper.

2 Whisk together 5 tablespoons olive oil with the honey, fish sauce, vinegar and ginger.

3 Put the pasta in the boiling water, return to the boil and cook for 2 minutes if using fresh pasta and 8–10 minutes for dried.

4 Heat the remaining oil in a large frying pan, add the pumpkin seeds and fry for 1 minute. Drain with a slotted spoon. Add the scallops to the pan and fry quickly for 2 minutes or until lightly coloured on the underside. Turn them over and cook for a further 2 minutes.

5 Reserve a small ladleful of the pasta water. Drain the pasta and return to the saucepan with the reserved pasta water. Add the rocket or watercress and a little salt and pepper and mix until the leaves just start to wilt. Transfer to warm serving plates and add the scallops. Spoon over the dressing and scatter with the pumpkin seeds.

Penne with swordfish and garlic crumbs *Using*
a meaty textured fish such as swordfish in a main-course pasta dish
means you can easily stretch a couple of large steaks to serve four.

PREPARATION TIME: 10 minutes

COOKING TIME: 25 minutes

SERVES: 4

75 g (3 oz) ciabatta

5 tablespoons olive oil

2 garlic cloves, crushed

150 g (5 oz) sugar snap peas, sliced diagonally

250 g (8 oz) dried penne

400 g (13 oz) swordfish steaks

250 g (8 oz) mascarpone cheese

finely grated rind of 1 lemon and 1 tablespoon juice

4 tablespoons chopped flat leaf parsley

salt and pepper

1 Tear the bread into small irregular pieces. Heat 3 tablespoons oil in a frying pan and add the garlic. Fry for a few seconds, stirring to break it up, then add the bread. Fry gently, stirring frequently, for about 3 minutes or until pale golden. Tip on to a plate. Blanch the peas in a small pan of boiling water for 1 minute.

2 Bring a large saucepan of salted water to the boil and add the pasta. Cook for 8–10 minutes or until just tender. Meanwhile, heat the remaining oil in the frying pan. Season the fish on both sides and fry gently for 7–8 minutes, turning once, until cooked through. Transfer to a plate and use 2 forks to tear the fish into small pieces, discarding the skin.

3 Add the mascarpone to the frying pan. Reserve a couple of ladlefuls of the pasta cooking water then drain the pasta and return to the pan. Add a little of the reserved pasta water to the frying pan with the lemon rind and juice, parsley and a little salt and pepper and heat through gently.

4 Pour the sauce over the pasta, add the fish, sugar snap peas and half the garlic crumbs and heat through for 1 minute. Spoon on to warm plates and serve topped with the remaining garlic crumbs.

Fideua

This is a sort of Spanish pasta paella, made using spaghettini or spaghetti broken into short lengths instead of rice and, ideally, cooked in a paella pan.

PREPARATION TIME: 25 minutes

COOKING TIME: 30 minutes

SERVES: 4

½ teaspoon saffron threads

200 g (7 oz) raw peeled prawns

400 g (13 oz) skinned firm white fish, such as monkfish, halibut or hake, cut into large chunks

3 garlic cloves

5 tablespoons chopped parsley

250 g (8 oz) spaghettini

100 ml (3½ fl oz) olive oil

1 small onion, finely chopped

4 large tomatoes, skinned and roughly chopped

1 teaspoon paprika

1 litre (1¾ pints) fish or chicken stock

salt and pepper

1 Soak the saffron in 1 tablespoon boiling water. Season the fish with salt and pepper. Use a pestle and mortar to pound the garlic and half the parsley together.

2 Roll up half the pasta in a tea towel. Run the tea towel over the side of a work surface to break the pasta. Tip the pieces into a bowl and break the remainder.

3 Heat half the oil in a paella pan or large frying pan and gently fry all the fish, turning the pieces, until just cooked through. Remove with a slotted spoon.

4 Add the onion to the pan and fry gently for 3 minutes. Stir in the garlic and parsley mixture, tomatoes and the remaining oil and fry for a further 5 minutes until the tomatoes are soft and pulpy.

5 Add the paprika, stock and saffron and bring to the boil. Add the pasta and cook, uncovered, for 15 minutes until it is just tender. Add the fish and remaining parsley and reheat gently. Season and serve.

Fideua

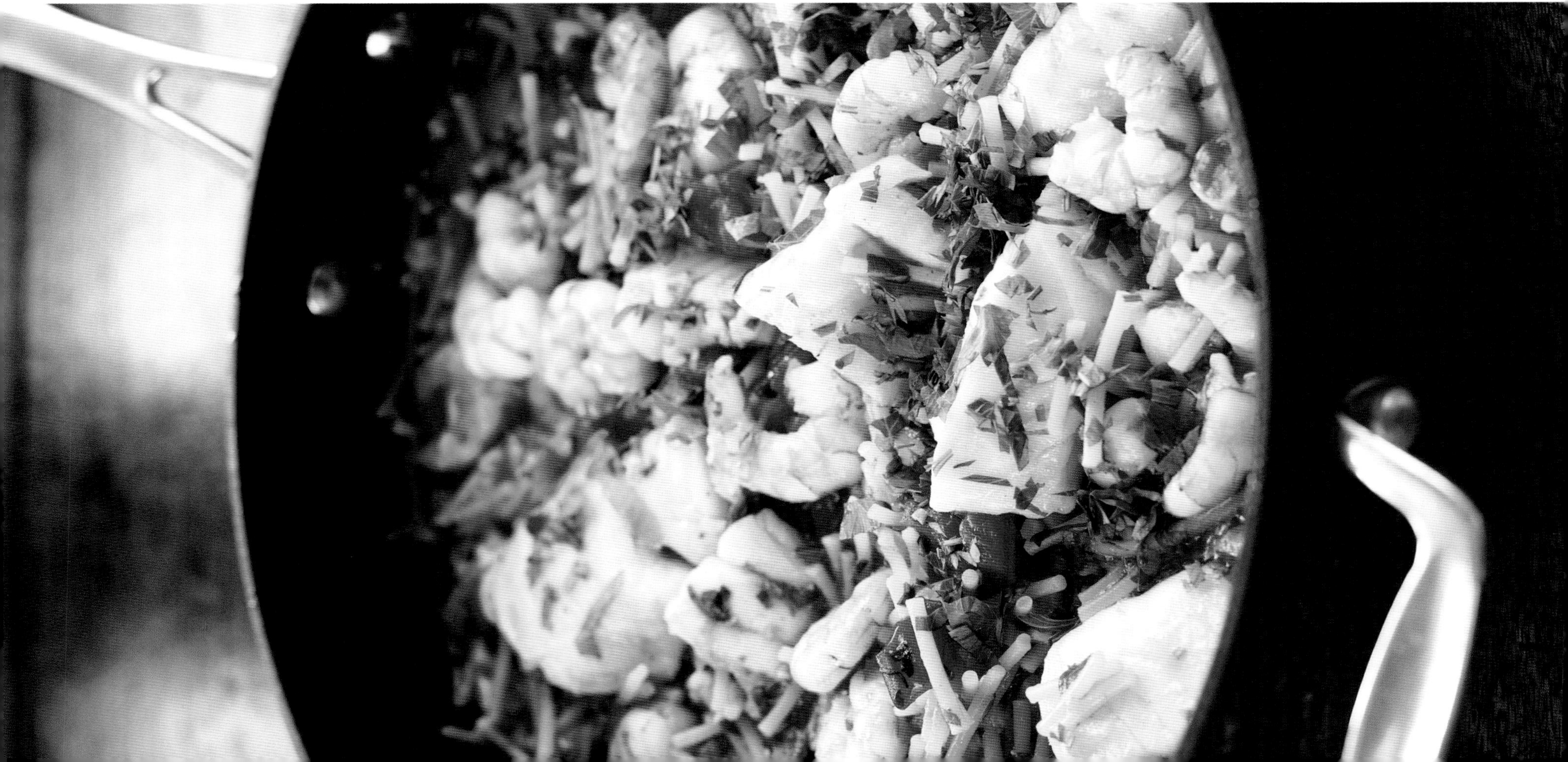

Mussel mouclade with conchiglie

The pasta soaks up all the deliciously creamy juices in this summery supper or lunch dish. Serve with a peppery salad, such as watercress or rocket.

PREPARATION TIME: 30 minutes

COOKING TIME: 25 minutes

SERVES: 4

1 kg (2 lb) fresh mussels

50 g (2 oz) butter

2 shallots, finely chopped

1 fennel bulb, finely chopped

3 garlic cloves, crushed

large glass of white wine

250 g (8 oz) fresh or dried conchiglie

2 tablespoons Pernod or other aniseed liqueur

150 ml (¼ pint) crème fraîche

4 tablespoons chopped fennel

salt and pepper

1 Clean the mussels, discarding any with damaged shells or open ones that do not close when tapped sharply with a knife.

2 Melt the butter in a large saucepan and gently fry the shallots and fennel for 6–8 minutes or until very soft. Stir in the garlic and cook for 1 minute. Add the wine and bring to the boil.

3 Tip the mussels into the pan, cover with a lid and cook for about 5 minutes until the mussels have opened, shaking the pan frequently. Drain through a colander into a large bowl to catch the juices. Return the juices to the saucepan, bring to the boil and boil until the liquid has reduced by about half. Remove about two-thirds of the mussels from their shells, discarding any that have not opened. Meanwhile, bring a large saucepan of salted water to the boil, ready to cook the pasta.

4 Add the pasta to the boiling water, return to the boil and cook until just tender, allowing 2–3 minutes for fresh pasta and 8–10 minutes for dried.

5 Stir the Pernod, crème fraîche, chopped fennel and all the mussels into the saucepan and heat through gently. Season to taste with salt and pepper. Drain the pasta and return to the pan. Toss with the sauce and serve immediately in shallow dishes.

Cracked pepper pasta with seafood

This is an incredibly pretty dish with saffron-tinted pasta, vibrant cherry tomatoes and glistening shellfish.

PREPARATION TIME: 45 minutes

COOKING TIME: 20 minutes

SERVES: 4

glass of white wine

1 teaspoon saffron threads

500 g (1 lb) clams or mussels, cleaned

4 tablespoons lemon-infused olive oil

4 garlic cloves, chopped

200 g (7 oz) squid rings

400 g (13 oz) raw peeled prawns

400 g (13 oz) cherry tomatoes, halved

4 tablespoons chopped parsley

1 quantity cracked pepper-flavoured pappardelle (see page 10)

salt and pepper

1 Put the wine in a large saucepan, crumble in the saffron and bring to the boil. Tip in the clams or mussels, cover with a lid and cook for 5 minutes, shaking the pan frequently until the shells have opened.

Drain through a colander into a large bowl to catch the juices. Bring a large saucepan of salted water to the boil.

2 Heat the oil in a large frying pan, add the garlic and cook for 30 seconds. Add the squid and fry for 3–4 minutes until the squid has puffed into rings. Remove with a slotted spoon. Fry the prawns in the pan until pink. Remove with a slotted spoon.

3 Add the strained cooking juices to the frying pan, bring to the boil and cook for a few minutes until slightly reduced. Stir in the tomatoes and the fish and heat through until the tomatoes have softened. Season to taste and stir in the parsley.

4 Tip the pasta into the water, return to the boil and cook for about 2 minutes until tender. Drain and return to the pan. Toss with the sauce and serve.

Silhouette noodles with lemon sole *This recipe sandwiches fragrant herb leaves between wafer-thin sheets of homemade pasta, creating a stunning silhouette effect.*

PREPARATION TIME: 45 minutes, plus drying

COOKING TIME: 10 minutes

SERVES: 4

1 quantity pasta dough (see page 8)

about 15 g (½ oz) small leaf herbs, such as basil, tarragon, chervil or flat leaf parsley

100 g (3½ oz) butter

2 large lemon sole, filleted, skinned and cut into chunks

2 tablespoons salted capers

1 tablespoon lemon juice

salt and pepper

1 Line 2 trays with flour-dusted tea towels or kitchen paper. Thinly roll out the pasta dough, using a machine or by hand, following the method on page 9. Very lightly brush one sheet of dough with water and arrange the leaves over the dough. Lay another sheet of rolled dough over the pasta and press down gently. Repeat with the remaining pasta sheets.

2 Reroll the dough, again using the machine or by hand, until it is fine enough to see the herbs clearly through the pasta. Cut into 2.5 cm (1 inch) wide strips. Transfer the strips to the trays and leave to dry for 30 minutes.

3 Bring a large pan of salted water to the boil. Melt half the butter in a frying pan. Season the fish with salt and pepper and fry gently for 3–4 minutes. Add the capers.

4 Put the pasta in the boiling water, return to the boil and cook for 2 minutes until tender. Drain, return to the pan and gently toss with the fish and capers. Pile on to warm serving plates.

5 Melt the remaining butter in the frying pan and stir in the lemon juice. Season and drizzle over the pasta.

Bottarga with spaghetti

Bottarga is salted fish roe, usually tuna or mullet. It can be bought in Italian delicatessens, either in a piece or ready grated, for sprinkling over pasta.

PREPARATION TIME: 5 minutes

COOKING TIME: 10 minutes

SERVES: 2

175 g (6 oz) fresh or dried spaghetti

6 tablespoons extra virgin olive oil

2 tablespoons chopped parsley

2 teaspoons chopped lemon thyme

2 garlic cloves, crushed

4 tablespoons grated bottarga

salt and pepper

1 Bring a large saucepan of salted water to the boil and add the pasta. Return to the boil and cook until just tender, allowing 2–3 minutes for fresh pasta and 8–10 minutes for dried.

2 Meanwhile, put the olive oil, parsley, thyme, garlic and plenty of black pepper into a small saucepan and heat gently for 2 minutes to flavour the oil.

3 Drain the pasta and return it to the saucepan. Stir in the flavoured olive oil, pile on to serving plates and sprinkle with the bottarga.

Herb farfalle with salmon and spicy salsa

For the freshest flavour, it's best to make your own herb-flavoured pasta, and for this recipe a coriander-flavoured pasta is ideal.

PREPARATION TIME: 25 minutes

COOKING TIME: 20 minutes

SERVES: 4

3 tablespoons light muscovado sugar

1 tablespoon lightly crushed cumin seeds

½ teaspoon dried chilli flakes

3 tablespoons lime juice

2 avocados, finely diced

4 tablespoons avocado oil, plus extra for drizzling

350 g (11½ oz) skinned salmon fillet

200 g (7 oz) runner beans, trimmed and sliced

1 quantity herb-flavoured farfalle (see pages 10 and 11)

salt and pepper

coriander leaves, to garnish

1 Heat the sugar in a saucepan with the cumin, chilli and 3 tablespoons water until the sugar dissolves. Bring to the boil and boil for a few minutes until syrupy. Stir in the lime juice and diced avocados.

2 Bring a large saucepan of salted water to the boil, ready to cook the pasta. Heat the oil in a frying pan, add the salmon and fry gently for 5 minutes on each side, or until cooked through.

3 Put the runner beans in the pasta water and return to the boil. Add the pasta, bring back to the boil and cook for 2 minutes until tender. Drain and return to the pan. Flake the salmon into the pan with the cooking juices and mix well.

4 Pile the pasta on to serving plates and spoon the salsa over it. Drizzle with a little oil and scatter with coriander.

Vegetables *Vegetarian pasta dishes take full advantage of all the fabulous different cheeses, from creamy mild ones such as ricotta, to fontina with its irresistible melting qualities, and the intensely flavoured Parmesan. Combining them with lightly cooked vegetables, tomato sauces, herbs and spices or crispy breadcrumb toppings provides an exciting range of flavour, colour and texture.*

You can add further variety with your choice of pasta, choosing silky smooth fresh pasta for serving with vegetables with bite, or firmer textured ones such as orecchiette, or wholemeal pasta for tomato-based sauces. Flavoured pastas such as cracked pepper or mushroom, either bought or homemade, can add further depth to the dish.

Goats' cheese and pepper lasagne *Meat-free*

lasagnes can be just as flavour packed as meaty ones. The creamy goats' cheese sauce is lovely against the tangy flavours of the peppers.

PREPARATION TIME: 30 minutes, plus soaking and cooling

COOKING TIME: 1 hour

SERVES: 4–5

50 g (2 oz) dried porcini mushrooms

225 g (7½ oz) spinach

4 tablespoons olive oil

1 large onion, sliced

2 red peppers, deseeded and roughly chopped

3 garlic cloves, sliced

2 x 400 g (13 oz) cans chopped tomatoes

4 tablespoons sun-dried tomato pesto

2 tablespoons chopped oregano

300 g (10 oz) soft goats' cheese

1 quantity Béchamel Sauce (see page 64)

200 g (7 oz) dried lasagne sheets

50 g (2 oz) breadcrumbs

salt and pepper

1 Soak the mushrooms in 200 ml (7 fl oz) boiling water. Wilt the spinach.

2 Heat 2 tablespoons oil in a saucepan and fry the onion and peppers for 5 minutes. Add the garlic, tomatoes, pesto, oregano, spinach, mushrooms and their soaking liquid and salt and pepper. Bring to the boil and simmer gently for 10 minutes.

3 Beat the goats' cheese into the béchamel sauce. Spoon one-quarter of the vegetable sauce into a shallow, 1.5 litre (2½ pint) ovenproof dish. Spread with one-quarter of the béchamel sauce. Arrange one-third of the pasta sheets over the sauce, trimming or breaking them to fit.

4 Repeat the layering, finishing with béchamel sauce. Toss the breadcrumbs with the remaining oil and scatter over the sauce. Bake in a preheated oven, 190°C (375°F), Gas Mark 5, for 45 minutes or until golden.

Goats' cheese and pepper lasagne

Pasta gratin with caramelized onions *The combination of sweet onions, melting cheese and smooth pasta sauce is creamy, comforting and easy to eat in this simple gratin.*

PREPARATION TIME: 10 minutes

COOKING TIME: 50 minutes

SERVES: 4

2 tablespoons olive oil

450 g (14½ oz) red onions, thinly sliced

1 teaspoon caster sugar

2 teaspoons chopped thyme

300 g (10 oz) dried penne or conchiglie

150 g (5 oz) Gruyère cheese, grated

75 ml (3 fl oz) crème fraîche

1 quantity Béchamel Sauce (see page 64)

salt and pepper

1 Bring a large saucepan of salted water to the boil, ready to cook the pasta. Heat the oil in a large frying pan and gently fry the onions for 10 minutes, stirring frequently, until pale golden. Stir in the sugar and thyme and cook for a further 5 minutes until lightly caramelized.

2 Meanwhile, put the pasta in the water, return to the boil and boil for 8–10 minutes or until tender.

3 Drain the pasta and spoon half into a shallow, 1.8 litre (3 pint) ovenproof dish. Scatter the onions over the top and cover with the remaining pasta. Mix up the pasta and onions slightly with a fork.

4 Stir half the cheese and all the crème fraîche into the béchamel sauce in a saucepan and heat gently until smooth. Spoon the sauce over the pasta and sprinkle with the reserved cheese. Bake in a preheated oven 190°C (375°F), Gas Mark 5, for 30 minutes or until bubbling and golden.

Pumpkin ravioli

The filling for this dish is delicious but very soft and creamy, so it is not a good make-ahead dish because the pumpkin will gradually dampen the pasta.

PREPARATION TIME: 40 minutes, plus drying

COOKING TIME: 50 minutes

SERVES: 4

450 g (14½ oz) pumpkin or squash, cut into small chunks, skin and seeds discarded

3 tablespoons olive oil

½ small onion, finely chopped

1 garlic clove, crushed

25 g (1 oz) amaretti biscuits, crushed

50 g (2 oz) cream cheese

plenty of freshly grated nutmeg

1 quantity pasta dough (see page 8)

flour, for dusting

75 g (3 oz) butter

1 teaspoon finely chopped rosemary

2 tablespoons chopped parsley

finely grated rind of 1 lemon and 1 tablespoon juice

salt and pepper

1 Put the pumpkin or squash into a small roasting tin and drizzle with half the oil. Roast in a preheated oven, 200°C (400°F), Gas Mark 6, for 30–40 minutes until tender. Leave to cool.

2 Heat the remaining oil in a frying pan and fry the onion until softened. Add the garlic and fry for a further 1 minute. Mash the cooled pumpkin in a bowl until pulpy. Beat in the onion, garlic, crushed biscuits, cream cheese and nutmeg. (Alternatively, whiz the lot together in a food processor.) Check the seasoning.

3 Line 2 trays with flour-dusted tea towels or kitchen paper. Roll out the pasta using a machine or by hand, following the method on page 9. Use the pasta dough and pumpkin mixture to make ravioli, following the method on page 12. Leave on the floured trays to dry for 30 minutes before cooking.

4 Melt the butter in a small saucepan and stir in the herbs, lemon rind and juice and black pepper. Bring a large pan of salted water to the boil. Cook the ravioli, in 2 batches, for 3–5 minutes. Drain well and pile on to warmed serving plates. Drizzle with the herb butter to serve.

Aubergine cannelloni

Although a little fiddly to prepare, this dish is well worth the effort, making a delicious combination of creamy ricotta filling and sweet, grilled aubergines.

PREPARATION TIME: 30 minutes

COOKING TIME: 50 minutes

SERVES: 4

4 sheets fresh or dried lasagne, each about 18 x 15 cm (7 x 6 inches)

2 medium aubergines, thinly sliced

4 tablespoons olive oil

1 teaspoon finely chopped thyme

250 g (8 oz) ricotta cheese

25 g (1 oz) basil leaves, torn into pieces

2 garlic cloves, crushed

1 quantity Fresh Tomato Sauce (see page 66)

100 g (3½ oz) fontina or Gruyère cheese, grated

salt and pepper

1 Bring a saucepan of salted water to the boil. Add the lasagne sheets, return to the boil and cook, allowing 2 minutes for fresh and 8–10 minutes for dried. Drain the sheets and immerse in cold water.

2 Place the aubergines in a single layer on a foil-lined grill rack. (You may need to do this in 2 batches.) Mix the olive oil, thyme and salt and pepper and brush over the aubergines. Grill until lightly browned, turning once.

3 Beat the ricotta with the basil, garlic and a little salt and pepper. Thoroughly drain the pasta sheets and lay them on the work surface. Cut each in half. Spread the ricotta mixture over the sheets, right to the edges. Arrange the aubergine slices on top. Roll up each piece.

4 Spread two-thirds of the tomato sauce in a shallow ovenproof dish and arrange the cannelloni on top. Spoon over the remaining tomato sauce and sprinkle with the cheese. Bake in a preheated oven, 190°C (375°F), Gas Mark 5, for 20 minutes or until the cheese is golden.

Pasticcio

This is a general term for a combination of pasta and other ingredients, baked together in a sort of pie. Like most bakes, it can be assembled in advance, ready for reheating.

PREPARATION TIME: 20 minutes

COOKING TIME: 40 minutes

SERVES: 5–6

400–500 g (13–16 oz) cheese-filled or other vegetarian tortellini

250 g (8 oz) broccoli florets, cut into bite-sized pieces

225 g (7¼ oz) cream cheese

200 g (7 oz) crème fraîche

150 g (5 oz) smoked mozzarella, grated

1 quantity Fresh Tomato Sauce (see page 66)

25 g (1 oz) breadcrumbs

4 tablespoons grated Parmesan cheese

salt and pepper

1 Bring a large saucepan of salted water to the boil. Add the tortellini, return to the boil and cook for about 5 minutes until tender. Remove with a slotted spoon.

2 Cook the broccoli in the pasta water for 3 minutes or until slightly softened. Drain thoroughly.

3 Heat the cream cheese and crème fraîche in a saucepan, whisking until softened and the consistency of pouring cream. Stir in three-quarters of the mozzarella and plenty of black pepper. Layer the pasta, broccoli and tomato sauce in a 1.8 litre (3 pint) pie dish.

4 Pour over the cheese sauce so it runs down between the pasta and vegetables. Sprinkle with the remaining mozzarella, then the breadcrumbs and Parmesan. Bake in a preheated oven, 180°C (350°F), Gas Mark 4, for 30 minutes until pale golden.

Spaghetti with tomato pangriatata

This is a really simple dish with fragrant bursts of lemon thyme, the rich flavour of sun-dried tomatoes and mild, melting cheese.

PREPARATION TIME: 10 minutes

COOKING TIME: 15 minutes

SERVES: 2

50 g (2 oz) breadcrumbs

4 tablespoons extra virgin olive oil

several sprigs of lemon thyme

50 g (2 oz) sun-dried tomatoes in olive oil, thinly sliced, plus 2 tablespoons oil from the jar

25 g (1 oz) basil leaves, plus extra to garnish

1 tablespoon white wine vinegar

150 g (5 oz) fresh or dried spaghetti

125 g (4 oz) baby mozzarella, halved

salt and pepper

1 Bring a large saucepan of salted water to the boil, ready to cook the pasta. Tip the breadcrumbs into a small frying pan with 1 tablespoon olive oil. Pull the thyme leaves from the stalks and add them to the pan.

2 Whiz the oil from the sun-dried tomatoes, plus the remaining olive oil and the basil leaves in the food processor. Briefly blend in the vinegar and a little salt and pepper.

3 Cook the pasta, allowing 2–3 minutes for fresh and 8–10 minutes for dried.

4 Heat the frying pan containing the breadcrumbs and cook, stirring, until golden and crisp. Stir in the tomatoes.

5 Drain the pasta and return it to the pan. Add the basil dressing and mozzarella. Toss the ingredients until the mozzarella starts to melt then pile on to warm serving plates. Sprinkle with the crumbs and serve scattered with extra basil.

Mushroom tagliatelle with gremolata

Gremolata is a mixture of herbs, lemon rind and garlic. It's used to bring a burst of lively, aromatic flavour to this dish.

PREPARATION TIME: 30 minutes, plus drying

COOKING TIME: 10 minutes

SERVES: 4

1 quantity mushroom-flavoured pasta dough (see page 11)

15 g (½ oz) dried porcini mushrooms

50 g (2 oz) butter

4 tablespoons olive oil

1 small onion, finely chopped

200 g (7 oz) chestnut or button mushrooms, thinly sliced

4 tablespoons chopped herbs, such as parsley, tarragon, fennel or basil

finely grated rind of 1 lemon

2 garlic cloves, finely chopped

salt and pepper

Parmesan cheese, grated, to serve (optional)

1 Use the pasta dough to make tagliatelle, following the method on page 10. Leave to dry. Put the porcini mushrooms in a bowl, cover with boiling water and leave to stand for 15 minutes.

2 Melt the butter with 1 tablespoon oil in a frying pan and fry the onion for 3 minutes until softened. Drain the soaked mushrooms. Thinly slice the porcini mushrooms and add them to the pan with the chestnut or button mushrooms and a quarter of the herbs. Fry gently for 5 minutes.

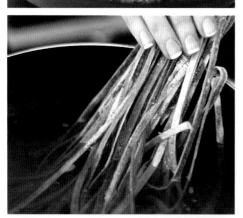

3 Mix the remaining herbs with the lemon rind, garlic and plenty of black pepper.

4 Bring a large saucepan of salted water to the boil. Add the pasta, return to the boil and cook for about 2 minutes until tender. Drain and return to the saucepan. Add the mixture from the frying pan and toss the ingredients with the remaining oil. Transfer to warm serving plates and serve with the gremolata.

Mushroom tagliatelle with gremolata

Wholewheat pasta with chicory, taleggio and pears

Creamy taleggio cheese, stirred through hot pasta, makes an irresistibly stringy, melting sauce.

PREPARATION TIME: 15 minutes

COOKING TIME: 15 minutes

SERVES: 4

275 g (9 oz) wholewheat rigatoni or penne

75 g (3 oz) unblanched hazelnuts, roughly chopped

4 tablespoons hazelnut or walnut oil

2 red chicory, halved and cut into thin wedges

1 red onion, sliced

2 small pears, peeled, cored and cut into wedges

2 teaspoons pink or green peppercorns in brine, drained and rinsed

250 g (8 oz) taleggio cheese, diced

salt and pepper

chopped parsley, to sprinkle

1 Bring a large saucepan of salted water to the boil. Add the pasta, return to the boil and cook for 10–12 minutes until just tender.

2 Meanwhile, heat a large dry frying pan, add the hazelnuts and cook, shaking the pan, until they start to toast. Remove from the pan. Add the oil to the pan and gently fry the chicory and onion until they begin to brown. Lift out with a slotted spoon and fry the pear slices lightly on each side. Use a pestle and mortar to crush the peppercorns lightly.

3 Drain the pasta and return it to the saucepan. Add the peppercorns, chicory, onion, pears and cheese and stir for 2–3 minutes, off the heat, until the cheese starts to melt. Pile on to warm serving plates and scatter with the toasted nuts and parsley.

Pasta primavera
This is a great recipe to make with spring vegetables. This version has a little pesto stirred into the sauce, giving it a lift without detracting from the fresh flavours of the vegetables.

PREPARATION TIME: 20 minutes

COOKING TIME: 20 minutes

SERVES: 4

100 g (3½ oz) baby carrots

125 g (4 oz) fresh broad beans

150 g (5 oz) fresh peas

200 g (7 oz) asparagus tips

25 g (1 oz) butter

1 fennel bulb or 4 baby fennel, thinly sliced

275 g (9 oz) fresh tagliatelle or pappardelle

300 ml (½ pint) double cream

3 tablespoons pesto

salt and pepper

Parmesan cheese, grated, to serve

1 Bring a large saucepan of salted water to the boil and cook the carrots for 3 minutes or until softened. Add the beans and peas to the pan and cook for a further 2–3 minutes until just tender. Add the asparagus tips and cook for a further 1 minute. Lift out all the vegetables with a slotted spoon, reserving the water.

2 Melt the butter in a large frying pan and gently fry the fennel for 5 minutes.

3 Return the vegetable water to the boil and add the pasta. Bring back to the boil and cook for 1–2 minutes until tender. Drain and return to the pan.

4 Add the cream, pesto and a little salt and pepper to the frying pan and heat through for a couple of minutes. Tip the sauce into the pasta pan with all the vegetables and toss together. Pile on to warm serving plates and serve scattered with grated Parmesan.

Tagliatelle with spicy pea fritters
These little split pea fritters are quite hot and spicy, so halve the spices for a milder flavour. They can be made in advance and kept in the refrigerator.

PREPARATION TIME: 30 minutes, plus soaking

COOKING TIME: 40 minutes

SERVES: 4

300 g (10 oz) split yellow peas

1 onion, roughly chopped

25 g (1 oz) breadcrumbs

2 garlic cloves, chopped

1 tablespoon crushed cumin seeds

¾ teaspoon dried chilli flakes

several sprigs of mint

1 egg

8 tablespoons lemon-infused olive oil

25 g (1 oz) butter

200 g (7 oz) dried tagliatelle

200 g (7 oz) roasted red peppers, thinly sliced

4 tablespoons chopped coriander

salt and pepper

1 Put the peas in a large bowl, cover with cold water and leave to soak overnight. Drain and put in a saucepan. Cover with cold water, bring to the boil and cook for about 25 minutes until tender. Drain.

2 Tip into a food processor with the onion, breadcrumbs, garlic, cumin seeds, chilli, mint, egg and salt and pepper and blend to a smooth paste. Shape firmly into small balls, about 2.5 cm (1 inch) in diameter.

3 Bring a large saucepan of salted water to the boil, ready to cook the pasta. Heat half the oil with the butter in a large frying pan. Add the pea fritters and fry gently, stirring, for 5 minutes or until golden.

4 Add the pasta to the water, return to the boil and cook for about 10 minutes until just tender. Drain and return to the saucepan. Stir in the peppers, coriander, pea fritters and remaining oil and mix together gently to serve.

Pasta with spicy lentils

This dish has a slightly sweet and sour flavour, which gives an appetizing lift to the slightly earthy flavour of the lentils. Use any dried pasta shapes with this dish.

PREPARATION TIME: 10 minutes

COOKING TIME: 45 minutes

SERVES: 4

200 g (7 oz) black or Puy lentils

1 litre (1¾ pints) vegetable stock

3 bay leaves

1 onion, quartered

250 g (8 oz) plain or spinach-flavoured dried pasta

5 tablespoons mild olive oil

2 small courgettes, thinly sliced

250 g (8 oz) cherry tomatoes, halved

1 red chilli, thinly sliced

2 tablespoons clear honey

2 tablespoons coarse grain mustard

1 tablespoon lemon juice

25 g (1 oz) mixture of parsley, mint and chives, finely chopped

salt

1 Rinse the lentils and put them in a saucepan with the vegetable stock, bay leaves and onion. Bring to the boil, reduce the heat to its lowest setting and cook gently for about 20–25 minutes or until the lentils are tender and the stock has been absorbed or almost absorbed.

2 Bring a large saucepan of salted water to the boil. Add the pasta, return to the boil and cook for about 8–10 minutes or until just tender.

3 Heat 1 tablespoon oil in a frying pan and fry the courgettes until golden. Add the tomatoes and fry for a further 1 minute to soften them slightly.

4 Beat the remaining oil with the chilli, honey, mustard and lemon juice.

5 Drain the pasta and return to the pan. Drain the lentils of any unabsorbed stock and tip them into the pasta pan, discarding the onion quarters. Add the courgettes, tomatoes, dressing and herbs and toss all the ingredients together. Check the seasoning and serve warm.

Gnocchi verdi

This type of gnocchi, sometimes known as Roman gnocchi, uses a semolina base rather than the more familiar potato. It's soft and creamy comfort food!

PREPARATION TIME: 50 minutes, plus cooling

COOKING TIME: 30 minutes

SERVES: 4

75 g (3 oz) butter, plus extra for greasing

1 litre (1¾ pints) milk

200 g (7 oz) semolina flour

100 g (3½ oz) Parmesan cheese, grated

3 egg yolks

350 g (11½ oz) spinach

plenty of freshly grated nutmeg

2 shallots, finely chopped

150 ml (¼ pint) single cream

salt and pepper

1 Grease a 30 x 23 cm (12 x 9 inch) or similar-sized baking dish and line with baking parchment. Put the milk in a large saucepan and bring to the boil. When the milk starts to boil, lower the heat and sprinkle in the semolina flour, in a steady stream, whisking well until the mixture is very thick. Continue beating until the mixture is almost too thick to beat and starts to come away from the sides of the pan.

2 Remove the pan from the heat and dot with 25 g (1 oz) butter, half the Parmesan and then the egg yolks. Season with salt and pepper and beat until combined. Turn the mixture into the tin and spread in an even layer with the back of a spoon or palette knife. Leave for at least 30 minutes until cool and set.

3 Put the spinach in the cleaned pan with 1 tablespoon water and a generous sprinkling of nutmeg. Cover and cook briefly until the spinach has wilted.

4 Use a 5 cm (2 inch) round cutter to cut the gnocchi into rounds. Chop the trimmings and scatter them in a shallow, 2 litre (3½ pint) ovenproof dish. Spoon the spinach on top. Arrange the gnocchi rounds, slightly overlapping, on top.

5 Melt the remaining butter in a frying pan and fry the shallots until softened. Stir in the cream and spoon over the gnocchi. Scatter with the remaining Parmesan and bake in a preheated oven, 200°C (400°F), Gas Mark 6, for 20 minutes until pale golden.

Index

Acknowledgements

Photography: © Octopus Publishing Group Ltd /Stephen Conroy

Executive Editor Sarah Ford
Editor Charlotte Macey
Executive Art Editor and Design Tim Pattinson
Senior Production Controller Manjit Sihra
Food Stylist Joanna Farrow
Props Stylist Liz Hippisley

The publisher would like to thank the following suppliers for the loan of kitchen equipment for photography:

David Mellor www.davidmellordesign.co.uk

Divertimenti www.divertimenti.co.uk

Hansens Kitchen Equipment www.hansens.co.uk